A Portrait of the Parish of Foveran

Published by South Minnes Publications

Janet Jones

Printed on 130gm^2 Silk Art

Typeset in Palatino 10.5pt. Printed by Halcon Printing, Stonehaven.
Cover designed by Zoe Sadler B.A. (Hons. 2004) a graduate of the University of Dundee.
Zoe studied illustration at Duncan of Jordanstone College of Art.

ISBN 0-9550814-0-8

"A Portrait of the Parish of Foveran" was funded by the Foveran Partnership with a grant from 'Awards for All.'

ACKNOWLEDGEMENTS

Without the generosity of all these people, this book would not have been possible. Particular thanks to Bob Stewart of Newburgh for lending me so many of his photographs, Douglas Flett for writing about Udny Station, Violet Garrick for her memories of Mill of Fiddes and Christine Fordyce for her recollections of Foveran Public Hall.

Richard Argo
Chris and Jim Aiken
Ed Aiken
Sandy & Norma Anderson
Karen Berry
Pat Booth
Eric and Lena Buchan
Charlie Catto
Jennifer Craig
Lorna & Ian Cruickshank
Mary Cumming
Bob Davis
Annabel Drysdale
Ina and John Duncan
Mom Dunnet
Charles Esson
Mrs Esson
Marc Ellington
Pearl Elrick
Eveline Emslie
Keith Fenwick
Dick Fleming
Douglas Flett
Audrey Forbes
Christine Fordyce
Violet Garrick
Bill Gallacher

Martyn Gorman
Neil Gow
Doug Gray
Allan Green
Alex Green
J. R. Hume
Sandy Ingram
Bill Johnston
Madge Kinghorn
Hazel Marr
Jeanette Meecham
Amy Miller
Lorna McKen
William Mackie
Sandy MacDonald
Jeanette Meecham
Elaine Moffat
June Marshall
Moira Massie
Rose Moroney
John Ollason
Sandy Penny
Dave Rafaelli
Linda Ramsay
Barbara Reid
Eric Reid
Bill and Sheila Robertson
Alex Ross
Pam Ritchie
Zoe Sadler
Johnston Sangster
Doig and Liz Scott
Stuart Seivwright
Alistair Sinclair
Carolyn Smith

Ian Stephen
Bob Stewart
Jim & Elizabeth Strachan
Gerald Stranraer-Mull
Ian and Betty Stott
Mrs M. Stott
Ann and John Stuart
Hazel and Alfie Stuart
Norman Thompson
Bill Wood
Betty Wood
Margot Wright
Newburgh-on-Ythan Golf Club
Press & Journal Library
Aberdeen City Archives
Aberdeen City Library
Marischal Museum
The Aberdeen Maritime Museum
Ellon Library
The National Museums of Scotland
Special thanks to the librarians at the Central Library, Old Meldrum for their help and patience.
Great North of Scotland Railway Association.
Mitchell Library, Glasgow
R.C.A.H.M.S.
Buchan Heritage.
Aberdeenshire Heritage
National Archives of Scotland
Press & Journal
Culterty Field Station
Newburgh S.W.R.I.
Aberdeen Art Gallery
Foveran School
Cultercullen School
Newburgh School

CONTENTS

Newburgh 1950s.   Photograph courtesy of Bob Stewart.

The Parish of Foveran lies about 9 miles north of Aberdeen. On the east, it extends 1½ miles along the sea coast to the mouth of the river Ythan. To the north the Burn of Tarty separates it from the parish of Logie Buchan, and the river Ythan divides it from the parish of Slains. To the west is the parish of Udny and to the south is the parish of Belhelvie. It is roughly 6 miles long from east to west and between 3 and 4 miles wide.

At the beginning of the 14th century there were five baronies within the parish. There was Foveran, from which the parish gets its name, Tillery and Pitmillan, all belonging to the Earls of Buchan. After the Battle of Barra in 1314, Robert the Bruce gave all this land to William de Strabrok of Aberdeen in gratitude for his support.

In 1359 Foveran, together with Tillery and Pitmillan, passed to the knightly house of Turing, a family of Norman extraction. They retained the lands for the following three centuries and were responsible for building a castle which incorporated the legendary Turing Tower. The name Foveran is thought to have come from the Gaelic "fueran" meaning "well of the springs" and refers to the spring which still flows close to the site of the old castle, no trace of which now remains.

The Turings were succeeded by the Forbes of Tolquhon and it was during their ownership that the Turing Tower fell down. In the 1750s, the lands of Foveran were bought by the Robertson family and it was Andrew Robertson who set about building the present Foveran House using stone from the ruined tower and castle.

The other two baronies were Knockhall and Fiddes. Knockhall, also known as the barony of Newburgh, belonged to the Earl Orkney and the Lords Sinclair. In 1633 the lands were bought by John Udny of Belhelvie and have remained in the possession of the family ever since. During the 14th century, the barony of Fiddes passed from the Earls of Buchan to the family Fothes or Fiddes who retained ownership for the following two hundred years. The land then went to Lord Forbes followed by Sir James Crichton of Frendraught before being bought around 1640 by the present owners, Udny of Udny.

These days there are four settlements within the parish, Newburgh, Cultercullen, Foveran and Udny Station.

Much the largest is Newburgh with a population of around 1392. In days gone by it was a busy port with most of the residents working in and around the village. Now, although there is some employment in local businesses, most people have to travel in to Aberdeen to work. The weather in the parish is much the same as in other places in the north east of Scotland with an extra twist for Newburgh. At times, while the rest of the parish is bathed in sunshine, the haar descends. It comes in as a wall of mist from the sea engulfing the estuary and the village in a cold damp shroud which can remain for two to three days. Only a mile inland, the temperature might be 18 degrees while in Newburgh it is only 10. That apart, Newburgh is a very pleasant place to live. There is a wonderful sense of space with the beach, the river and Forvie Nature Reserve all within walking distance. There is an 18 hole golf course, two excellent hotels, a general store, a hairdresser, a butcher's shop, a church, a post office, Aberdeen University's Culterty Field Station and Oceanlab, some small businesses and a very good primary school.

Unlike so many places within commuting distance of Aberdeen, where the original villages have disappeared under a sea of housing estates, Newburgh is still relatively intact and has a strong sense of community. If anything, the incomers since the oil boom in the 1970s and 1980s have benefited the village by ensuring the school has a good intake of pupils and that the clubs and societies thrive. Over recent years, there have been various attempts by building firms to increase the number of houses but these have been vigorously opposed by almost everyone.

The area within the parish known as Foveran takes in Foveran Church and Foveran School and a number of the surrounding farms. Most people live in or around Blairythan Terrace where there is the Public Hall, the football pitch and the children's play park. The park equipment was provided by a community fund raising effort in the 1990s.

Cultercullen is the smallest of the settlements. Like Foveran, it covers the houses around the school and some adjacent crofts and farms. Pupils come to school from an area covering Udny Station to the west, Damhead to the east, Logierieve House to the north and Leighs of Cannahars to the south.

Udny Station is the youngest of the villages having grown up around the railway which was established in 1861. At the beginning of the 20th century there were fewer than fifty inhabitants.

There is a Community Centre, built by people in the village in the 1980s, where a range of activities such as the WRI, dancing and meetings take place. Unfortunately the shop and the bank had to close in the 1980s but there is still a part-time post office, the Udny Station Hotel, the surgery, and the garage run by Albert Lamb.

The steam train pulling in to Udny Station.

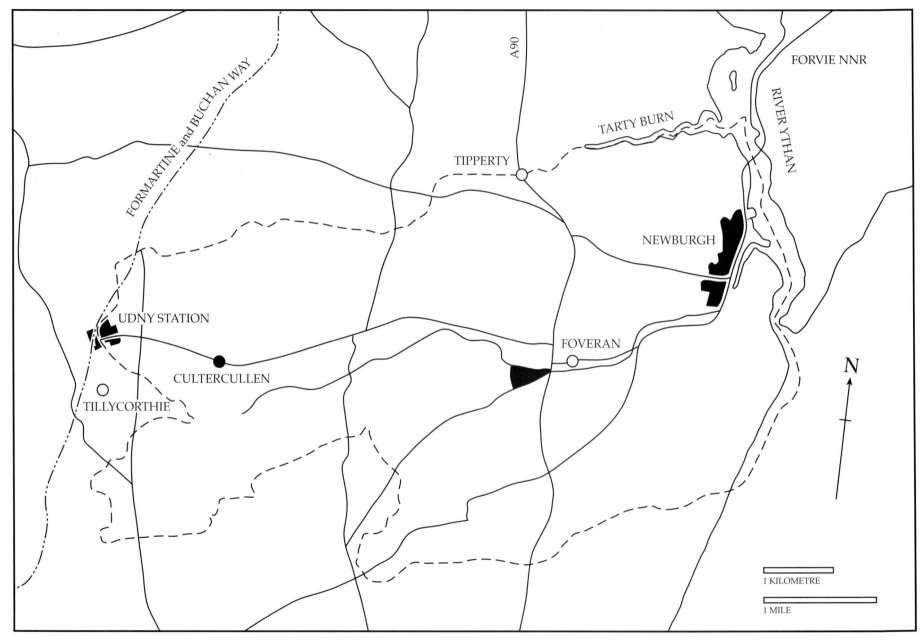

FORMARTINE and BUCHAN WAY

A90

FORVIE NNR

TARTY BURN

RIVER YTHAN

TIPPERTY

NEWBURGH

UDNY STATION

FOVERAN

CULTERCULLEN

TILLYCORTHIE

N

1 KILOMETRE

1 MILE

Map by A.A. Anderson.

N E W B U R G H

As early as the 15th century Newburgh had a regular shipping trade bringing in timber from Norway and taking out wool.

It is likely the port could have done more business if, during the 16th and 17th centuries, Aberdeen and other Scottish burghs hadn't operated certain restrictive practices which discouraged the expansion of trade. These practices included not allowing foreign ships to bring in goods unless to a free port and, if they did, the local merchants claimed the exclusive right to buy the cargo, no doubt at rock bottom prices.

Newburgh came under the jurisdiction of Aberdeen and in 1573, when the magistrates got to hear that ships from Norway and other places were unloading goods at Newburgh as if it was a free port, they were outraged. When their pockets and privileges were affected, they took action and ordered an armed party to go to the port and arrest and immobilise the ships by confiscating their sails.

In common with most ports of any importance from the late 1700s onwards, Newburgh had a Seamen's Society which operated for the benefit of its members and their dependants. The Newburgh Shipmaster's Friendly Society, founded 4th November 1799, afforded "weekly Allowances in money to Members during sickness and inability for labour, till they complete their 65th year." It also provided for the widows of men lost at sea and their children up to 12 years of age.

Records of payments in and out of the Society's funds and the list of members were kept under lock and key in the Seaman's Box. In March 1834, when the Society in Newburgh held a special meeting to amend some rules in the constitution, Alexander Sinclair was President, Andrew Cameron Vice President, William Allan Treasurer and Thomas Mitchell was Clerk.

The "Despatch" and the "Emma Louise".   Photograph courtesy of Dick Fleming.

The Quay circa 1900.   Photograph courtesy of Dick Fleming.

The Newburgh Traction Engine Company circa 1900.   Photograph courtesy of Dick Fleming.

The "Anno" under construction.   Photograph courtesy of Aberdeen Maritime Museum.

From around the 1800s, trade in Newburgh became less hampered by rules and regulations imposed from Aberdeen and, in common with other small ports such as Portsoy and Fraserburgh, cheerfully got on with the business of both legal and illegal trading.

Attracted by cheap dues, boats bringing in lime and coal and taking out grain came into the port regularly. And the smugglers thrived - the "James" of Newburgh was noted for carrying duty free spirits. (The appointment of a coastguard in the 1800s helped to restore Newburgh's reputation as a respectable port.)

The following notice which appeared in "The Aberdeen Journal" 26 March 1806 gives an indication of the growing importance of Newburgh as a port.

FISHERMEN AND PILOTS
WANTED
For the Town and Harbour of NEWBURGH, at Ythan Mouth.

SIX or EIGHT stout FISHERMEN and PILOTS who have been bred and employed as Whitefishers for some years past, and are willing immediately to engage with the heritor, Capt. Udny, for a certain period, to serve as Fishermen and Pilots, where very great encouragement will be received both for the sale of their Fish, and employment as Pilots - the profits of which are very considerable, from the increased number of shipping which now daily frequent that harbour.

The tenants will also have the advantage and privilege of gathering what is commonly called Slug, or Buckie Bait, within the flood-mark of the water of Ythan; and from purchasing from the tenant of the mussel fishing, what quantity of Mussels they may further have occasion to use as Bait only, upon payment to him of the low rate of 4d per peck, during the time of their engagement. They will likewise

Inside the iron foundry and smithy operated by John Rae sited just along from the quay.

Dick Fleming.

The "Anno" at the quay.   Photograph courtesy of Bob Stewart.

have the benefit of Dwelling Houses to each, and a Fishing Boat, upon payment to the heritor of a reasonable rent; or, if they provide Houses and Boat upon their own expense, they will be entitled to the right of Fishing and Pilotage, during the period they may agree upon with the heritor, free of any rent whatsoever, except the tiend *fifth, and 1s for each fisherman.

For further particulars, such persons as are desirous of further Information, may apply to A. Carnegie, advocate, Aberdeen; or to Mr John Black in Watridgemuir; or George Thomson, Esq. Ythan Lodge.

*tiend: tithe

The lack of a pier before the middle of the 19th century was a problem so all loading and unloading had to be done at low tide. Horses and carts were brought alongside the vessels, the horses often suffering by having to stand for long hours in the freezing water.

A survey report by M. Gibb in 1819 suggested developing the mouth of the Ythan with buildings for storing grain, ship building yards and houses for fishermen and seamen but nothing came of it.

There must have been at least one ship building yard in Newburgh around the time Gibb wrote his report because records show that ship owner John Black commissioned three, if not four, ships to be built there. These were vessels which traded around Britain and also took emigrants to Canada.

Black commissioned the schooner "Helen" in 1815 and under Captain George Legatwood, she had one crossing to Quebec with 11 passengers in 1816. He also commissioned two other ships, the brig "Pilot" in 1818 which crossed from Aberdeen to Miramichi/Saint John with 7 passengers in 1822 and the "Ythan" which under Captain Alexander Craigie made two crossings with 23 passengers from Aberdeen to Halifax/Miramichi in 1816 and 1817.

The "Anno".

The only remaining granary which stored grain awaiting shipment.

Whether Black commissioned the brig "Juno" is not known. She was however built in Newburgh and made one crossing from Aberdeen to Quebec in 1819 with 6 passengers.

In 1841, a wooden pier was built at the Inches making the process of loading and unloading much safer and more efficient. Incoming cargo was transferred directly on shore or on to lighters or barges of 6 - 8 tonnage and taken further upstream to Ellon. In the early days these lighters were propelled by men using poles, sometimes sail, but mainly by the tide. There were various stopping places on the way where goods could be discharged.

Alternatively, goods could be unloaded into large trailers and hauled inland on the turnpike road by The Newburgh Traction Company to places such as Old Meldrum. This was a cheaper goods service than that of the Great North of Scotland Railway.

One of the earliest ships to use the new pier was the Aberdeen Lime Company's three masted schooner "Alexander Nicol". She was the last Aberdeen-built sailing ship to trade from Newburgh.

Towards the end of the 19th century, the paddle tug "Despatch" came into service and it became possible for several lighters to be pulled at once. She was also used to assist in berthing Mitchell & Rae's steamers, "Ruby" and "Gem" and continued working until 1924 when it made more economic sense to transport all goods by road.

Newburgh has always had two disadvantages as a port, the Ythan bar and the shallowness of the river. In order to maintain a channel deep enough for shipping, dredgers such as the "Rockchime" and the

All that remains of the "Karemma" which ran aground on the 21st of April 1976.

The "Christian" which ran aground on Christmas Eve 1987.   Photo Sandy Anderson.

"Sandchime" were used. Poles placed in the river indicated the navigable channel. Even with dredgers however, groundings were not infrequent.

In 1908 for example, the Aberdeen Lime Company's "Portlethen" ran aground at the bar while coming in with a cargo of basic slag before being pulled off by the lifeboat's towing tractor and in 1966 the Hull Gates' Shipping Company's "Paullgate" became stranded at the mouth of the river.

On the 21st of April 1976, the salvage vessel "Minto" was towing the Leith trawler "Karemma" to Fraserburgh when both boats ran aground at the mouth of the estuary. It was three weeks before anyone realised that several hundred gallons of diesel had leaked into the estuary. The hull of the "Karemma" can still be seen today.

And many Newburgh residents still remember seeing the hull of the coastal tanker "Christian" looming over them in the estuary when she became stranded on Christmas Eve 1988.

Mill owners Mitchell & Rae owned several ships on the Ythan. Their first coastal steamers were the "Gem", built 1878, and the "Ruby" (1882) and in 1913, the John Duthie Ship Building Co. built the single hatch coaster "Tillycorthie" for Mitchell & Rae. Her captain, Robert Soang, found her difficult to handle in the river and was always concerned she would run aground. The "Tillycorthie" was torpedoed and sunk in 1917 off the coast of Northumberland while sailing north with a cargo of coal.

The steam coaster "Udny Castle" was also built for Mitchell & Rae. She was sold not long after coming into service as her running costs were too high and she proved to be too big for the river. The "Emma Louise" from Bristol, pictured in the photograph with the "Despatch", was sold as she proved unable to cope with the rigors of the North Sea.

The shallow drafted "Anno" was built for Mitchell & Rae by Messrs. Hall Russell & Co in 1952 and is still remembered in Newburgh. She was named after the daughter of John Duguid, the mill's manager.

The "Anno" gave good service despite needing two new engines. She carried between 10,000 and 12,000 tons of cargo annually and, with her Captain James Cowie and crew of seven, brought in anthracite from South Wales and took oats and barley out. Grain was discharged directly from the granary on the quay into her hold at a rate of 40 tons an hour. In 1963, the "Anno" was sold to owners in Hull and renamed the "Spring Heather". Two years later she hoisted the Norwegian flag and became a sand carrier at Kopervik.

Between 1963 and 1968, Mitchell & Rae chartered the motor coaster "Ashdene" to bring in coal and take out grain. Her last call in 1968 marked the end of several hundred years of trade from the port of Newburgh.

Between the wars, Dutch and German steamers were frequent visitors to the Ythan bringing in locust bean, basic slag, bones and manure and taking out oats. The Dutch skippers often brought their families with them and, much to the amusement of the locals, were prepared to eat eider duck. Ian Cruickshank recalls that when a Dutch boat came into Newburgh, the young men in the village would try to get down to the quay to buy cheap beer and cigarettes before the customs man arrived. He also remembers that just as war broke out, the Dutch skippers painted the hatches of their boats in the colours of the Dutch flag to assert Holland's neutrality

There has been no commercial shipping on the Ythan since 1973 when Mitchell & Rae closed down.

The two boats alongside are the "Ruby" and the "Gem" and the small tug in the background is the "Despatch". The hulk on the right is the "Queen". W.F.S. 1886.

Alexander Robb. Coxswain (1938-1965).   Photo courtesy of Bob Stewart.

Service Board.

Alexander Charles and William Aird.
1882. Smack 'Conquerer' of Newburgh. Rescued 2.
1889. Jan. 28. Steam Trawler 'Gannet' of Granton. Rescued 8.

Ellen Newman and John Bentley.
1889. Nov. 22. Brig 'Olga' of Ronne. Rescued 7.
1891. Mar. 5. Small boat of Aberdeen. Rescued 1.
1894. Nov. 26. Steam Trawler 'Lionel' of South Shields. Rendered Assistance.
1894. Dec. 20. Steam Trawler 'Bonito' of Aberdeen. Rescued 8.

James Stephen No. 19.
1905. Jan. 27. Steam Trawler 'Ulundi' of Grimsby. Stood By.
1908. Dec. 17. Steam Trawler 'Tillydrine' of Dundee. Rescued 8.
1910. Dec. 6. Steam Trawler 'Taymouth' of Aberdeen. Rescued 8.
1911. Nov. 30. Steam Trawler 'Bass Rock' of Leith. Rescued 9.
1912. Feb. 9. Steam Trawler 'Lord Ashby' of Blyth. Rescued 4.
1912. Feb. 15. Steam Trawler 'Faith' of Aberdeen. Rescued 8.
1915. Oct. 30. Barque 'Erikijesson' of Skudesnoes. Rescued 6.
1923. Jan. 20. SS 'Portlethen' of Aberdeen. Rescued 7.
1923. Oct. 19. Steam Trawler 'Imperial Prince' of Aberdeen. Rescued 7.

John and Amy.
1926. June 7. 'Johann Georg'. Rendered Assistance. Landed 15.
1928. Feb 25. Steam Trawler 'Isle of Wight' of Hull. Rescued. 10.
1934. Feb. 14. Steam Trawler 'Shandwick' of Aberdeen. Rendered Assistance.

John and Robert C. Mercer.
1935. Sept. 27. Steam Trawler 'Ebor Abbey' of Aberdeen. Rescued 5.
1940. Feb. 9. Motor Vessel 'Auchmacoy' of Newburgh. Rescued 6.
1941. Mar. 28. 'Melrose Abbey' of Hull. Rescued 47.

John Ryburn.
1943. April 2. FV 'True Vine' of Aberdeen. Rendered Assistance.
1947. Aug. 21. SS 'Holdernook' of Hull. Landed 12.
1956. Dec. 29. Steam Trawler 'Lombard of Grimsby'. Rendered Assistance.
1957. Mar. 1. Motor Vessel 'Ferm' of Sweden. Rescued 19.

Station closed September 1965.

The crew of the "John & Amy" 1926-35.
G. Park, J. Grey, G. Duncan, A. Moir, G. Mitchell, R. Walker, W. Duncan, A. Youngson, D. Benzie, W. Wood, Cox. John Innes, B. Logan, J. Youngson, W. Youngson, G. Elder, J. Innes, J. Keith, J. Rae, J. Park.

Newburgh Lifeboat Coxswains.

1877-1895   Robert Mutch

1897-1908   James Walker

1908-1931   John Innes

1931-1938   Alexander Youngson

1938-1965   Alexander Robb

30th September 1965 Lifeboat Station closed.

Newburgh Lifeboats.

"Alexander Charles and William Aird". November 1877. 30ft. 8-oared pulling and sailing boat.

"Ellen Newman and John Bentley". 1889. 31ft. self righter. Cost £300. Cox: Robert Mutch.

"James Stephen No 19". 1901. 34ft. by 7ft. self righter pulling and sailing. Cost £670.

"John and Amy". January 1926. 34ft. by 8ft. pulling and sailing boat. Cost £600.

"John and Robert C. Mercer". April 1935. 34ft. by 8ft. self righter.

"John Ryburn". 23rd June 1941. 32ft. by 9ft. Surf Class motor boat. Cost £3791.

Photograph courtesy of Bob Stewart.

The "Alexander Charles and William Aird."   Photograph courtesy of Bill Wood.

Launching the lifeboat.   Photograph courtesy of Bill Johnston.

Newburgh's lifeboats and crews have a proud history.

Early records are patchy and there are no records of lives saved from around 1827/28 when a local boat was modified and stationed at the mouth of the Ythan.

In 1877, Newburgh became a full Institution station with the launching of the "Alexander Charles and William Aird" and a boathouse costing £300 was built at the same time. It was a major event for the local community and spectators from the village and surrounding areas came to watch the new boat slip from her carriage into the water. Detachments from Collieston, Belhelvie and Bridge of Don gave a demonstration of coastal rocket apparatus as the crew rowed the boat up the river.

In the early days, launching the lifeboat involved most able-bodied people in the village, men and women alike. The boat on its carriage had to be pulled from the boathouse to the river or, depending on the location of the ship in distress, dragged along either the north or the south side of the estuary for launching off the beach.

In January 1878, the lifeboat went to the aid of a Peterhead schooner and a ship from Liverpool. The schooner was found abandoned and the ship did not require assistance. The first lives were saved in November 1882 when the "Conquerer", a local boat laden with coal, ran ashore at midnight when it tried to enter the estuary. Although the boat was breaking up in heavy seas, the lifeboat succeeded in rescuing both crewmen.

In 1889, the steam trawler "Gannet" of Granton became stranded on the north bank of the river. At 2a.m. on the 28th of January, the lifeboat rescued the crew of eight and brought them safely back to Newburgh the following morning.

"Ellen Newman & John Bentley"   Photograph courtesy of The Ythan Hotel.

"Robert and John C. Mercer"   Photograph courtesy of Bob Stewart.

In 1889, Newburgh was presented with a new lifeboat, the "Ellen Newman and John Bentley", a 7ft. 3" self righter rowing ten oars.

In November of that year, she was called out to assist the "Olga of Roone" which was stranded on a sandbank south of the Ythan. The lifeboat managed to rescue five men before the coxswain made a run ashore to pick up a fresh crew as by then his own men were exhausted. The Captain of the brig and another crewman were rescued. One man died however when he was hit by a spar.

Further successes included the rescue of the lone occupant of the "Alexander Duthie" in March 1891 and a salvage operation on November 1984 when the steam trawler "Lionel of South Shields" ran aground on the beach north of the estuary. The lifeboat crew helped to pass lines to the tug which was pulling the trawler clear of the sands. Again, in 1894, from the steam trawler "Benito" of Aberdeen which had become stranded at the bar, the lifeboat rescued eight crewmen.

"The James Stevens No 19" came into service in Newburgh in 1901 under coxswain James Innes. She cost £670 and was a self-righting 34ft. pulling and sailing boat. In her 25 years of service, she was called out 18 times and saved 53 lives.

In December 1908, this lifeboat rescued a crew of eight from the steam trawler "Tillydrine" of Dundee and in 1910 a further eight from "Taymouth" of Aberdeen. Nine were saved from the trawler "Bass Rock" of Leith in 1911, as were four of the crew of the "Lord Ashby" of Blyth in February 1912 in a joint action with the Coastguard off Forvie Sands.

Any callout involved up to forty helpers to launch and recover the lifeboat

On the Links trying out the new tractor for pulling the lifeboat.   Photograph courtesy of Bob Stewart.

James Innes B.E.M. Bowman 1919-1951.

John Innes. Coxswain of the lifeboat 1908-31.
Photographs courtesy of Pearl Elrick.

and a further fourteen "wet" men working waist high in the freezing water to steady the boat until she cleared the beach. It was cold, hazardous and exhausting work.

In the 1920s, women were paid sixpence for assisting in a launch and were given a sash to indicate that they were pullers. The lifeboat men drew an allowance of 5/- for a callout.

Further successful rescues were carried out from the trawler "Faith" in 1912 and the "Erikijesson" in 1915.

Coxswain Innes and Petty Officer Essam were awarded the Silver Medal for gallantry and Bowman James Innes the Bronze Medal after an outstanding rescue in October 1923 from the "Imperial Prince" of Aberdeen. The trawler had run aground near the Blackdog Rock and the Newburgh lifeboat was dragged seven miles along the sands before being launched opposite the wreck. Two men were rescued but a third was washed out of the lifeboat and drowned. Coxswain Innes then returned to the shore, picked up a fresh crew and returned to pick up a further five men who by then had been clinging to the rigging for thirteen hours.

In 1926, the pulling and sailing boat "John and Amy" came into service and in her nine years answered only three calls. One of these however was the steam trawler "Isle of Wight" which became stranded in thick fog at the mouth of the Ythan in February 1928. It was Coxswain Innes' last life saving callout before he retired in 1931. The crew of 10 was brought safely ashore.

Alexander Youngson followed as Coxswain and he took command of the "John and Robert C. Mercer" which came to the station in 1935. He served during seven relatively uneventful years for the lifeboat.

Launching the "John Ryburn" for the first time on the 23rd of June 1941. Photographs Bob Stewart.

The "Ferm" of Gothenberg stranded on the north side of the river in March 1957. 19 men rescued.

Alexander Robb became Coxswain in 1938 and served until the station closed in 1965. In 1940, a year after the outbreak of war, the "John and Robert C. Mercer" went to the aid of the "Auchmacoy" of Newburgh which had run aground at the mouth of the river. The crew of six was saved.

The biggest rescue in the station's history was in March 1941. The Belhelvie Coastguard reported a vessel in distress near the mouth of the Ythan. The weather conditions were appalling so it was decided to launch the lifeboat into the river and row over the bar.

The ship, the SS "Melrose Abbey", a vessel of 1900 tons and a crew of 49, had been driven off course while in convoy. On the first trip, the lifeboat brought 16 men ashore then returned to pick up a further 31. The remaining two men were picked up by the L.S.A.

The "John Ryburn" came on station in 1941. Costing £3791, it was the station's first motor-powered boat and was specially designed to work in broken surf and rough shallow water. Sadly, soon after its arrival, the station's only disaster involving loss of life occurred.

On the 26th of January 1942, phone lines were down and the roads were blocked by fallen trees and driving snow. As heavy seas pounded the bar, the SS "Lexrix" of London was driven ashore at Hackley Head. Communications were poor due to the bad weather and at first Newburgh was informed that the vessel was close to Cruden Bay and the crew would not be required. Some hours later, when it became clear that Hackley Head was the scene of the disaster, the "John Ryburn" was launched into the river.

The "Auchmacoy'" of Newburgh which ran aground at the mouth of the river in 1940.
Photo Bob Stewart.

The "Willie and May Gall" in Fraserburgh harbour 7th Sept. 2002.
Photograph courtesy of Richard Argo.

But there was nothing the lifeboat could do. The vessel was up on the rocks with her back broken and in the high seas the lifeboat could not approach. Coxswain Robb headed for home.

The lifeboat was only half a mile from home when a huge wave caught the port beam and capsized her. Five of the crewmen were thrown into the sea but the other two were trapped underneath. Although all the men were washed ashore some fifteen minutes after the boat turned over, assistant mechanic George White and crew member James Walker never regained consciousness. Alex Robb, William Wood, James Arthur, Eustace Williams and James Stewart were pulled clear of the water by Willie Gall who waded out into the freezing water to help.

To add to the tragedy, the "Lexrix" sank with the loss of 10 of her crew. Four were rescued by Dick Ingram from Collieston.

News of the disaster spread quickly through the village. As the snowdrifts were so deep on the north side of the river, the only way to retrieve the bodies of the two dead crewmen was to take a tractor and cart. On the approach to the bridge, a lone German bomber machine-gunned the cortège before dropping a single bomb. It missed the bridge, planed across the surface of the water and exploded in a roadside bank. The depression is visible to this day.

In 1947, the lifeboat took off 12 of the crew from the SS "Holderness" which had run onto rocks north of the Ythan, then stood by until high water.

In December 1956, the "John Ryburn" was pulled by tractor along the beach and launched to assist the trawler "Lombard" which had run aground south of the estuary. As the tide was carrying the vessel up onto the beach, it was decided to stand by until the trawler's crew could come ashore safely.

The naming ceremony of the "John Ryburn'" 23rd June 1941.   Photograph courtesy of Bill Wood.

The "John Ryburn's" last life saving service was in March 1957 when the "Ferm" of Gothenberg became stranded on the north side of the river. In the heavy swell, Coxswain Robb and his crew succeeded in rescuing all 19 crewmen.

The station closed in 1965. The lifeboat had been launched on service forty seven times and rescued 153 lives, a testimony to the courage and skill of her crews and the unwavering support of the people ashore.

Newburgh still has ties with the lifeboat. Mrs May Gall, widow of Newburgh builder Willie Gall, who pulled the crewmen ashore in January 1942, left £1,000,000 to the R.N.L.I. on condition that the money be spent in Scotland. Fraserburgh's new Trent Class vessel, the "Willie and May Gall" was bought with Mrs Gall's money.

Lifeboat House 2005.

The tractor that pulled the lifeboat in the late 1920s and 1930s. Alex Morrison and Geordie Willie Cruickshank. Photo Bob Stewart.

ROYAL NATIONAL LIFEBOAT INSTITUTION
(Supported entirely by voluntary contributions)

NAMING CEREMONY & DEDICATION
of Trent class lifeboat
'WILLIE AND MAY GALL'

at
PROVOST ANDERSON JETTY, FRASERBURGH
(adjacent to lifeboat station)
by kind permission of Fraserburgh Harbour Commissioners
on Saturday 7th September 2002 at 2.30pm
The lifeboat will be named by
MRS PATRICIA ARGO
The lifeboat was funded by the generous bequest of Mrs May Crombie Gall
plus other associated gifts.

Photograph courtesy of Richard Argo.

The Mill. Mitchell & Rae. From the left: The old kiln, the revolving kiln, the mill, the granary.
Photograph courtesy of Bob Stewart.

QUAY, WAREHOUSES, GRANARIES,
BONE MILL, &c., &c.,
AT NEWBURGH,
FOR SALE.
Reduced Upset Price, £3000.

There will be Exposed for Sale, by Public Roup, on FRIDAY, the 24th day of December current, at 2 o'clock, P.M., within the LEMON TREE TAVERN, Aberdeen,

THESE VALUABLE PREMISES. The NEW-BURGH COMMERCIAL COY., having resolved to Dissolve Partnership and wind up their Business, will be glad to treat with any party for their Premises at Newburgh, and Meadow of Waterton.

The Ground extends to about Six Acres, the Erections on which consist of a most substantial Quay, Bone Mill, with the necessary Machinery, and extensive Warehouses, Granaries, and other Offices, all laid down in the most commodious and suitable manner.

The Lighters and other Plant for carrying on the trade at Meadow will be disposed of at same time with these.

The Port of Newburgh—situated on the River Ythan, 13 miles North of Aberdeen—is almost the only Port betwixt that City and Peterhead, a distance of 33 miles, capable of admitting Coasting Vessels.

Peculiar advantages are thus afforded for communication with an extensive and fertile district of Country. At the Premises there has been for many years conducted an extensive business, capable of farther development, in the Import and Sale of Lime, Coal, Bones, Guano, &c., and the Export of Grain.

Application may be made to JOHN DUNCAN, Esq., Advocate; or NEIL SMITH, Jun., Merchant, Aberdeen; and Mr JAMES DYCE, at the Office in Newburgh, will show the Premises.

Meantime, these will continue open for the Sale of Lime, Coals, and Manure, and for the Settlement of Accounts due to the Company.

Aberdeen, Dec. 10, 1858.

Mr Alex Mitchell bought the premises.

Mr Alex Mitchell bought the premises in the late 1850s and a few years later went into partnership with John Rae from Ellon to form Mitchell & Rae. The firm became a limited company in 1912. The original mill, built on reclaimed land, was destroyed by fire in 1895.

The "Buchan Observer" reported the fire on the 31st December 1895.

"DAMAGE OVER £20,000.

Damage amounting to between £20,000 and £30,000 was caused by fire which broke out late on Monday night in the premises of Messrs Mitchell & Raè, grain and manure merchants, Newburgh, about 13 miles from Aberdeen. The flames, which were first observed issuing from the roof of the bone mill in the north end of the building were blown by a hurricane from the south-east. It was thought that this would be the means of saving a portion of the block, but so fierce was the conflagration that the fire forced its way against the wind and consumed the entire building. On the alarm being given, all the villagers turned out, but beyond pails no appliances were at hand, and little could be done to check the progress of the flames.

The steamer Gem, belonging to Messrs Mitchell & Rae, was lying at the quay in the river Ythan, a short distance from the works, but the hose-piping on board was not long enough to be of use in playing water on the burning buildings. The steamer pumped a supply of water from the river, however, and this was caught in large tubs, from which it was carried in pails and vessels of every kind to be thrown on the flames. These efforts were of little avail, and it was soon seen that, with the exception of several detached buildings, the extensive range was doomed. Several hundred tons of nitrate were stored on the premises, and as the fires reached this material, there was a continuous succession of great explosions. At five o'clock on Tuesday morning the buildings were practically destroyed, although the flames were raging up till noon. The damage is covered by insurance with the Royal Insurance Company."

Mitchell & Rae staff marking the retirement of the manager Mr John Duguid.
Photograph courtesy of Bob Stewart.

The Mill 2004.

By The 10th of January 1896, the "Aberdeen Journal" was able to report:

"MITCHELL & RAE PREMISES - THE RECENT FIRE. Although it is more than a fortnight since the conflagration took place here the fire in some parts continues to smoulder. It is conjectured that another week will elapse before it is altogether extinguished. As, however, it is now confined to one shed, the work of clearing away the debris is being actively prosecuted by a large staff of workmen, under the charge of Mr Forbes of Ellon. Mr Jenkins of Jenkins & Marr, has been to inspect the ruins, and it is generally believed that the work of reconstruction will be entrusted to his firm. The damaged manures, oats, barley, and feeding stuffs are being disposed of at various prices, regulated by the damage received. The firm's business is going on unchecked."

That same year the mill was rebuilt and greatly expanded. The work was carried out by the engineering firm Spencer & Co. from Wiltshire and was completed just in time for the harvest.

Even in 1897, it was an all electric granary, the first in the North East. A single 20 hp motor drove the whole plant. Huge conveyor belts stretched the length of the 240 ft. building, and with the help of special hopper units which could be moved along the belts and discharged on either side, the grain could be moved to any of the three floors and to any part of the building.

The Scottish Department noted in 1968 that there was an interesting system of fire breaks between the kiln, the mill and the granary. This may have prevented more damage when the mill went on fire in 1967.

The fire in December 1967 was started by a spark caused when the shaft on a high speed grinder broke. Nobody was hurt but the damage to the mill and the recently modernised machinery was estimated at over £60.000.

The fire in 1967.   Photograph courtesy of the P&J.

Up to 50 people from Newburgh and the surrounding area were employed by Mitchell & Rae so it was a very serious blow to the community when the firm closed in 1973.

MITCHELL & RAE LTD.
Agricultural Merchants & Shipowners
NEWBURGH
ABERDEENSHIRE

——oo——

Telegrams: Telephone:
Mitchelrae   25, 26, & 35
Newburgh, Aberdeenshire.   Newburgh, Aberdeenshire.

Local farmers sent their grain for hashing and there are still people in Newburgh who remember George Aiken from East Knockhall pushing a huge barrow of corn weighing several hundredweights to the mill to have it ground. The barrow was known locally as "Aiken's Transport". Mr Aiken was a great reader and on several occasions the library returned a pound note he had been using as a bookmark.

The firm stored, dried and milled grain, oats in particular. It exported oatmeal and grain, imported coal, hired out agricultural machinery, produced chemically-treated seed oats and owned and maintained several ships. There was also a mill at Stuartfield and a retail outlet in Ellon where Costcutters now stands.

Shovelling grain inside the granary 1949. Photograph courtesy of the P&J.

Flooding in Newburgh 1902.   Photograph courtesy of the P&J.   A view from the Gallow Hill 1930s.

A view from the Gallow Hill 1930s.   Looking over towards Inch Road and Mitchell & Rae 1910s.   Photo Dick Fleming

Eddie Forbes and Bill Burt at the salmon nets 1989.   Photograph courtesy of Audrey Forbes.

fish measuring 4ft 4" and weighing 70lbs caught in the Ythan in 1755, there was a record catch some five years later.

"There being 250 from one draught, all of which - except ten - weighed upwards of 30lbs." according to the "Aberdeen Journal". So much fish, however, brought about a glut on the market so prices were low.

Nowadays, the salmon and sea trout season lasts from the 11th of February until the 31st of October and no fishing is allowed on a Sunday.

There seems to be a pattern of good and not so good years and changes in the times fish are in the river. Doug Grey and Bill Wood recall that the salmon - or "reid fish" as they call it - used to return to the river in September. These days it can be as late as November. There was also a good Spring run of fish which is not the case now.

Reported minimum catches salmon and grilse with rod and line were 25 in 1979, 133 in 1982 and 15 in 1988. Catch numbers have risen in recent years due to changes in the management of the river introduced over the past twenty five years.

In 1978, Eddie Forbes was persuaded by Udny and Dudwick Estates, who own the fishing, to leave the Forvie Station and come to the Newburgh Station to manage both the rod and line and the commercial fishing. His brief was to improve conditions for anglers on the Ythan.

As far back as the 1600s, fishing on the Ythan has been regulated. In 1647, Thomas Forbes of Waterton was granted a commission to prevent the "slaughter of reid fish, smowtes and fray of all fishes" and anyone caught fishing was to be prosecuted. Two years later, a law was passed preventing any fishing at all between the 8th of September and the 1st of January.

Perhaps the regulations had some effect because not only was a monster

One of the boats for hire on the Ythan. Photograph courtesy of Audrey Forbes.

Newburgh Angling Club. Kevin Moir Trophy 20-06-92. Dave Fraser in foreground. Photograph Sandy Anderson

On the commercial side, where fish were caught in stake nets on the beach, wider mesh was introduced to enable sea trout to escape and by the late 1990s stake netting stopped altogether.

On the rod and line side, the number of anglers on the river was reduced. Up until 1989, it was possible to buy a day ticket at the Post Office and at weekends there could be as many as 150 fishermen on the river. A scheme whereby 21-year leases of a beat for a specified week in the year and a maximum of four rods on each beat was introduced, with some stretches being reserved for Newburgh Angling Club. Day tickets on local waters are still available but many fewer than in previous years.

The regulations are also much stricter. Fishing has to be by traditional methods with fly or spinning line and anglers are only allowed to keep a maximum of four sea trout and one salmon per day. It is also forbidden to keep any finnock, kelts or baggots or any fish shorter than 13 inches. River Watchers are authorised to inspect tackle and permits and any fish caught and to stop anyone using illegal equipment or methods.

Every year, eggs are stripped from some salmon and sent to a hatchery. When the fish are large enough, they are put into the burns around Newburgh and there are plans to do the same for sea trout.

Audrey Forbes took over as Fishing Manager in 1997 and has continued the conservation and restocking work of her late husband.

Until the 1950s, in the spring and summer many of the men in Newburgh worked in fishing-related jobs. The Udny Arms, for example, employed up to 12 ghillies to take guests out on the river. Often they fished at night and Bill Wood remembers seeing the lights from their boats bobbing in the water.

Eddie Forbes and Bill Burt with the jumper nets.   Photo courtesy of Audrey Forbes.

Ythan mussels.   Photograph courtesy of Bob Davis,

At the end of the summer, the ghillies would find work hairsting and in the winter they went darging (ditching) until the fishing season started again.

In the 1930s, Doug Grey found he could earn good money from November to February digging for lugworms which were used as bait for catching cod on the long lines. He got 2/6d per lb and could earn as much as £7 in a week.

Unlike Collieston, there has never been much coastal fishing from Newburgh, possibly because trading was more lucrative or perhaps because of the navigational difficulties presented by the river itself. In the 1950s both Donald Wood and Bob White went to sea but they were the exceptions.

For hundreds of years however, the mussels in the Ythan were vitally important as food for the table, as a commodity to be sold in Aberdeen and as bait.

The fishermen of Footdee, Torry and Collieston - and some of the Newburgh people - attached the mussels to the hooks on the long lines used to catch haddock, plaice, cod and whiting. The fish were either smoked, dried or salted then stored or sold. In Newburgh fish was often dried on the Links on "washing lines".

Up until the late 1920s, most of the people who lived in the small thatched cottages in Timmerlum Street were fisher folk. The women baited the hooks and cleaned and prepared the fish caught by the men. Then, wearing white aprons and with a laden basket on their backs, they walked to Ellon and the surrounding district to sell their wares. (Jessie McPherson describes them as "very religious, very kindly folk, mostly Bretheren.")

No. 1 Timmerlum Street. James and Mrs Crombie.   Photo Richard Argo.

Eddie Forbes mending nets.   Photograph courtesy of Audrey Forbes.

Women from other coastal villages such Collieston used to trudge along the cliff paths to Newburgh to collect mussels for use as bait. On their return, they laid them in rocky pools to keep fresh - that is, until the pier was built in 1894 and the foreshore became a beach.

Line fishing, and so the need for mussels as bait, began to decline in the 1930s when the coastal fishermen moved to larger boats in Peterhead and Aberdeen. Also herring fishing was becoming more important and nets rather than longlines were being used to catch white fish.

During the 1930s and 40s, the Udny Arms leased the mussel beds from Udny and Dudwick Estates and employed Jimmy Innes to manage them. He was extremely strong and could lift the big barrels full of mussels on to a lorry single handed.

Since the unfortunate siting in the 1970s of the sewage outfall in the middle of the mussel beds, the mussels are now inedible and the chefs in the Udny Arms can only wring their hands in frustration. Such a potential harvest and only the eider grow fat on it.

In days gone by, Ythan mussels were also a source of freshwater pearls. The Kellie Pearl, thought to be part of the Scottish crown jewels, came from a

freshwater mussel caught in the Ythan. Unfortunately, due to heavy exploitation from the 16th to the 19th centuries, and increased pollution in the 20th and 21st, the freshwater mussel is in decline.

The Salmon Bothy or Corf House.

Taking the nets in on the tractor.   Photograph courtesy of Audrey Forbes.

Eddie Forbes and Bill Burt 1989.   Photograph courtesy of Audrey Forbes.

Salmon nets or jumpers.   Photo Audrey Forbes.   Nets drying at the bothy.   A. Forbes.   The Ice House where fish was stored.

Newburgh 1950s.

War memorial and cemetery
dedicated on 15th Oct. 1922.

THE BOER WAR
"Aberdeen Journal" January 10th
1900.
"NEWBURGH
*The following officer and men of C Company
2nd V.B.G.H. have volunteered their services
for South Africa:- Lieutenant A. Harvey,
Sergeant Morrison, Private G. Morrison, W.
Main, W. Leslie, G. Brown and Wm.
Thomson; also ex-volunteers, through
Lieutenant Harvey - ex-Sergeant G. Greive,
ex-Corporal James Cochrane, and ex-
Privates James Harvey and Wm. Harper."*

"Aberdeen Journal" March 2nd after
the Relief of Ladysmith.
"NEWBURGH
*Glorious news received with general
rejoicing. Flags out and bells ringing.
Arranging for bonfire. The volunteers are to
be paraded on the Links and volleys fired."*

Photo courtesy of Christine Fordyce.

Private Jim Bruce,
15th Gordon Highlanders,
son of William and Margaret Bruce,
Fiddesbeg Cottages, Foveran.
Jim was killed in action in World
War 1 on the 8th of July 1916.
Jim was the second of
eleven children.

"Then again we've ae skipper - ye ken who I mean -
Who rammed wi' his trawler a Hun submarine:
Says he tae their Captain, a German baboon,
Ye're nae fit for men fae the Nee-bo-ro' Toon."

This verse appears in a poem printed in the Christmas card sent by the Reverend Thomas McWilliam in 1918 to his parishioners on active service. It refers to the contribution to the war effort made by the mine sweeping trawler "Dorothy Gray" commanded by Skipper A. Youngson R.N.R. from Newburgh.

On the 22nd of November 1914, the Grand Fleet left Scapa Flow in the Orkneys to search for submarines. On the 23rd of November, the U18 submarine passed into the Pentland Firth and continued on into Scapa Flow but when there was no sign of the Grand Fleet, came out again. It was then the U18 was spotted and rammed by the "Dorothy Gray".

With her hydroplane steering badly damaged, the U18 nose-dived, hitting the rocks on the seabed off Muckle Skerry. She then rose to the surface where her crew hoisted the white flag and surrendered to the destroyer "Garry".

The "Dorothy Gray" had the honour of being the first Auxiliary Patrol vessel to bring about the loss of a German submarine. Skipper Youngson and his crew received £500 and "Hearty Congratulations" from Admiral Colville, Admiral Jellicoe and the First Lord of the Admiralty.

In World War 1, Mitchell & Rae lost two of their colliers. The four-year old "Tillycorthie" was sunk by submarine gunfire off Northumberland and the "Ruby" was mined in the Orkneys.

January 2004.   Photograph courtesy of Lorna McKen.

January 2004.   Photograph courtesy of Martyn Gorman.

Between 1939 and 1945 most able bodied men in the parish either volunteered to join the forces or were conscripted. Only those in reserved occupations such as farming or who were not passed medically fit remained. Land girls and prisoners of war often replaced the farm workers who were called up.

When it was realised that the long, firm sandy beaches of northern Scotland were ideal landing sites for German troops and tanks, beach defences were put in place from the Forth to Wick. The man responsible for organising the construction of these defences was Chief Royal Engineer G. A. Mitchell, a veteran of World War 1. He is buried in Holyrood Cemetery in Newburgh.

Along the shore, there were barbed wire entanglements, pill boxes, arrays of interlocking tubular poles to prevent tanks from landing, gun emplacements armed with mock guns pointing out to sea, concrete blocks along the high water mark and on the Links, poles were driven into the sand to deter gliders.

Forvie was mined from the end of Greenhill to the bothy at Rockend and some nineteen of the bombs there have never been recovered, lost in the constantly shifting sands. Four mine-free pathways were made for local people to walk in safety.

When the pill boxes and concrete sea defences were being constructed, the contractor Tawse commandeered all useable tractors and carts to take cement to the site. Bill Wood remembers a big green Oliver 90 tractor being driven by James Robertson Justice. He was staying at the Udny Arms for the fishing and came to help.

Concrete defences on the estuary 2005.

A pillbox near Waterside Bridge 2005.

The photographs of the concrete blocks on page 34 were taken at New Year 2004 after stormy weather exposed some of the tank defences. A few days later they disappeared under the sand again.

When these blocks were newly cast, the men who made them sometimes scratched messages or their names in the wet concrete. The block shown on page 34, is signed by Louis Oliver, born 2nd of March 1910, and shows caricatures of Winston Churchill and Adolf Hitler.

The Home Guard patrolled the shoreline and the Links and kept a lookout for any sign of the enemy. There was Bill Mitchell from Mill of Ardo, Alec and John Cruickshank of Cruickshank and Rae, Sergeant Major Postie Watt, a veteran of the First World War, Willie Gall, John Duncan from Mill of Foveran and many others. Members would be on duty in the pill boxes two or three nights a week where telephones were installed should there be anything untoward to report. The men carried out exercises on the Links and used to march up and down carrying shotguns. (Most people in Newburgh owned guns in those days.)

One evening someone reported seeing suspicious footprints on the beach and the Home Guard patrolled all night looking in vain for the "spy" who had made them.

On Sundays, the voluntary workers from the Auxiliary Fire Service, Ambulance and First Aid Post, special constables and wardens would hold exercises on the Links with large crowds coming to watch. The Gordons, who were billeted at The Lodge at Collieston, also trained there.

Railings surrounding gardens and public buildings were taken away to be made into munitions. (The ones from the Church Hall were only replaced

2004.   Photograph courtesy of Martyn Gorman.

Remains of pillboxes where the Home Guard kept watch at night.

in 2003.) Trucks too were commandeered for the war effort. Cruickshank and Ross had only just taken delivery of two Albions when they were impounded. Some time later, one of the firm's drivers on service in France came across one of the trucks still in its blue and grey livery.

Newburgh was bombed on a number of occasions with Mitchell & Rae at the quay and the bridge being the targets. In an interview for "The Ellon Times", Mabel Aiken remembered how everyone got to know the particular sound of the German bombers coming over.

In 1940, a stray bomb landed in Charlie Catto's park at Mill of Newburgh, the impact cracking the ceiling in Sangster's Bakery on Main Street. In 1942 a bomb bounced on the water near to the quay and exploded close to the bridge at Waterside. This raid is described in more detail in the Lifeboat Section. Whether this was the occasion John Duguid, manager of Mitchell & Rae, pushed a young George Marshall from Meikle Haddo into his safe to protect him from the bombs, is not certain.

To prevent any lights showing which might have led to an air attack, windows had to have shutters fitted. Everyone carried their gas masks with them at all times and the lights on bicycles and farm vehicles were covered with hoods made of tin with three slits to allow only the minimum light. Ina Duncan from Mill of Foveran had to cross the road in pitch darkness to get to the parlour to do the milking.

After Norway was occupied, Aberdeen became the base for arming the North Atlantic fleet and the city was subjected to heavy bombing raids. The Germans would test their guns on their approach to Aberdeen and many a tattie field and line of fencing in Foveran was machine-gunned as a result.

Barbed wire beach defences to impede ground troops. The wire was laid out in 3 rolls stacked in a triangular shape and anchored into the sand at regular intervals with stout wooden posts or metal spikes. Most of the wire was collected at the end of the war. At the mouth of the Ythan some of the more substantial remains of the defences can still be seen.
Photograph and information courtesy of Martyn Gorman.

Concrete defences on the beach 2005.

Farmers were encouraged to grow as much food as possible. Flax was grown for the first time in Foveran to provide linseed oil for cattle and sheep.

During the war years, people in the parish were enthusiastic fund raisers for the Newburgh War Work Depot and other war-related causes.

In 1940, Mr and Mrs H. Edgar Smith from Culterty opened their bird sanctuary to visitors raising on one occasion £3 10/- 0d. Newburgh Musical Society gave recitals while Dr Ritchie from The Bungalow directed plays such as "Warthill's Courtship" and "Robin-a-Tiptoe" in the Public Hall.

Mrs Smith from Newburgh House and head of the local W.V.S. gave a practical lead to aluminium collection by starting a collection point in her garden.

Pupils from the school knitted blankets and Newburgh Sunday School sent their October collection in 1940 to help children in the bombed areas of London. In 1943 a group of young people performed two comedies, "The Ghost in the Corn Kist" and "Oor Geordie" written by local author Miss E. I. Keith. Dominie Lyall, who introduced the evening, announced that all proceeds would go to the Red Cross Agricultural Fund and Sunshine Homes for Blind Babies.

Foveran residents became very resourceful when it came to "make and do". At the W.R.I. in September 1940, Mrs B. Clark demonstrated how to make a pinafore dress from an old coat.

They also collected eider duck eggs to preserve in waterglass for baking and driftwood and the corks from fishing nets for kindling.

In 1944, some prisoners of war were being repatriated. In June of that year, Pte. J. Moir, Gordons, Chapel Croft, was among them. He was the guest of honour at a "Welcome Home Social" where Mrs Ritchie, Secretary of the War Work Party, presented him with a gift.

Towards the end of the war, a "Welcome Home Committee" with Dominie Lyall as chairman, was set up for those returning to the parish. Whist drives were popular fund-raisers, one being a match between Newburgh residents and the local farmers. (The farmers won on games and matches but there was a draw on tricks.)

In December 1945, a Fancy Dress Party held in the Public Hall raised £23 for the Welcome Home Fund. The prize winners were:

Children: Lorna Moir, Mary Christie, Donald Wood, Maurice Yeats, Betty Robb, Betty Duncan, John & Margaret Gavin and James Gibson.
Adults: M. Robb, C. Penny, N. Morrison, G. Cruickshank, B. Gillespie, B. Will, G. Forbes and G. Moir.

The war in Europe ended on the 8th of May 1945 and on the 2nd of September 1945 the Japanese surrendered.

The remains of the sea defences along the high water mark.

The remains of the interlocking tubular poles which were part of the anti tank defences.

A pillbox in the dunes.

Sangster the Baker.   Photograph courtesy of Hazel Stuart.

Before the days of supermarkets and easy access to Aberdeen, there were many more shops in Newburgh.

In the 1920s and 30s, there was Souter William Benzie, known as "Bangie Benzie" whose shop was where the Post Office is now. He made boots and thigh high waders in leather for the fishermen and held court in the back where he did repairs. His sister kept house for him.

Next door was Henry Ironside, the tailor who sat cross-legged as he worked. He was assisted by his daughter Mary who, as Mary Peters, kept the shop going as a haberdashery until the late 1980s. A small elfin figure, Mary sold buttons, cotton reels, thread, knitting wool, clothes and postcards. In winter she burned one piece of coal at a time in the grate and always knew exactly what was in every box on the tightly packed shelves.

Mary refused to go decimal so everything was labelled in old money.

One day three fishermen staying at the Udny Arms in July had such a cold day out on the estuary, they decided to go into Aberdeen in search of long johns. They had no luck in town but Mary was able to supply them with good old fashioned pink striped ones.

Then came the café run by Mrs Forbes and her daughter Mrs Dunbar. Visiting football teams and the home teams would go there for tea after matches.

There was Keith's Corner which sold sweeties and lemonade and some groceries. It was run by Jimmy Keith and his wife Bella. In the 1920s, Jimmy Keith would attract a large crowd to watch his annual swim across the Ythan at high tide.

Then there was Sangster the Baker. Bob Stewart remembers that he could always get a rowie by going in the side door when the shop was closed. Alex Sangster employed delivery man Benzie who took pride in getting through to remote farms whatever the weather. He didn't take kindly to the words "Oh I didn't think you'd make it today Benzie, so I've baked."

Hazel Stuart from Bridgefoot Farm remembers her great uncle Willie Brown, who was chief steward with the Aberdeen Steam Navigation Company, coming to tea with his sister Margaret Sangster and bringing with him his friend Alfred Hitchcock.

Further up on the same side of Main Street was Morrisons, a small general merchants run by Bella Morrison and her daughter. Johnnie Morrison was a postie.

Robert Taylor, tailor and professional golfer.   Photograph Bob Stewart.

Between the 1930s and 50s, dairy produce was delivered by the farms of Ythan Bank and Mill of Newburgh. Some families collected their milk directly after milking from the dairy at Firmohr on Inch Road.

In the 1920s, one of the cottages down Errol Place was a lodging house for travelling folk and was known as "Tinkies".

At the end of the lane is supposed to be the Inn in which the Chevalier de St. George, the Old Pretender, spent the night on the 24th of December 1715 on his way to Montrose where he embarked for France. There used to be a plaque on the house to commemorate the event but it has long since disappeared.

Coming back down Main Street opposite the Church Hall was Murray's

Stores, then Reid Brothers with the two butchers Alex Gillespie and Johnie Rae.

Down the lane was tailor Bob Taylor who was helped in the shop by daughter Jessie. He was also a professional golfer and in his obituary in 1927, he was described as a "finished golfer and a capital coach". He taught the Crown Prince of Siam when the Prince stayed at the Udny Arms in July 1898.

Fred MacPherson had the chemist shop where the Mace is now. He was a highly respected man who acted as doctor during the war. (If the doctor had to be called out, he came from Ellon on a motorbike and side car.) Fred had two daughters, Daisy and Jessie. Daisy worked in the shop while her sister helped their mother in the house. It was Jessie who wrote the essay "Newburgh-on-Ythan Yesterday and Today" to raise funds for Foveran Church.

Between the chemist and the Post Office was Mr Wood's butcher shop where John Park, helped by his wife Jeanie, was the butcher.

Over the years, Newburgh Post Office has moved a number of times up and down Main Street. Around the 1940s, it stood opposite the present one with Mr Imlach, or "Watchie Pym" as he was known, in charge. Helen Murray described him as "a very strict postmaster". On Pension Day he would retreat to the back shop with a customer's pension book where he placed the money between the pages before returning it to its owner. He kept a white cockatoo in a shed in his garden and local children came to chant "Come and dance. Come and dance" to make the bird jump up and down on its perch. Watchie Pym also sold fishing tackle, jewellery and clocks and was an excellent photographer.

Norman Mutch
M.P.S.

YTHAN PHARMACY
NEWBURGH

Telephone Newburgh 93

**UDNY ARMS
HOTEL**
NEWBURGH

Fishing on the River Ythan
Famous for Sea-trout
Permits and tackle obtainable at the Hotel

Tel. NEWBURGH 73

CHARLES CATTO
(Catto's Dairy)
Mill Of Newburgh

*Deliveries Daily
Orders Promptly
Attended To*

Telephone 77

**SPARK'S DAIRY
Firmohr
Newburgh**

T.T. Milk from Attested Herd

Your Guarantee of Quality

Telephone Newburgh 15

The Post Office then moved across the road to Notions shop where Rose Moroney was postmistress from 1980 until she retired in 2004. During her time, computers were introduced - a steep learning curve for someone who admitted she had used a slate and pencil at school. Fortunately for Newburgh, Morag Norrie took over from Rose and, unlike so many other villages in the 21st century, still has a Post Office.

Many people still remember Postie Andy Ewen with affection. He always felt that the three driving lessons he had before the Post Office gave him a van were not enough and would cheerfully admit to being a terrible driver. He much preferred doing his round on foot.

Back in the 1870s, long before Postie Andy, the postman was the diminutive Mr Hutcheon, or "Little Postie" as he was known. He walked from Cultercullen to Newburgh and back every day. It may be six miles each way as the crow flies, but a lot further with all the diversions to houses and farms on the way. When he retired in 1898, his round was taken over by the mail gig.

In the 1940s, there was the joiner known as "Dilly Do" who had two fingers on one hand and three on the other. Billy Well, who served his time with Willie, got a job in the shipyards in Aberdeen. This meant a bike ride in and out of the city every day. Eventually Billy became tired of doing this so joined the Navy.

In the 1930s, there were two builders, Wm. Gall and John Moir. William Gall's son, also called William, took over the business until he retired in the early 1980s. Willie was known in the village as "Red Gall" after touring collective farms in Russia and model schools in China during the 1960s. He regularly walked the beach and collected driftwood

For a short time, the Post Office was opposite the old Clydesdale Bank on the corner of Errol Place with Jimmy Gibson as postmaster then it moved back down the Main Street to where the Mace is today.

In the 1950s, Norman Mutch was postmaster and chemist followed by Jimmy Urquhart. There was a lady postmaster for a while until Davie Donald took over. Although Davie was the postmaster, more often than not it was Marjory, his wife, who was behind the counter. When the Donalds first took over, all mail was sorted and postmarked on the premises.

obsessively. People in the village still remember him staggering back from as far as Rockend carrying huge pieces of wood with his faithful mongrel Roger by his side.

One day in the early 1980s, Willie found the beach strewn with dressed planks of wood, jetsom from a passing ship. Despite a bad heart condition,

The Grocer's Cart 1886. William Fiddes Smith.

The Brewery Cart which passed every Tuesday. William Fiddes Smith 1886.

he ran back to the salmon house where he borrowed a tractor and trailer from Eddie Forbes. What happened to all the wood remains a mystery.

Willie was a very intelligent man who played the stock market so well, his widow was able to leave over a million pounds to buy the new Fraserburgh lifeboat. He also kept parrots and was eloquent on the subject of how much he disapproved of Princess Margaret and her lifestyle.

In her essay on Newburgh written in 1964, Jessie McPherson mentions Tammie Neil and his wife who, in times gone by, made "the best candy that was ever tasted and many a half-penny disappeared when Tammie produced his candy on Fridays. Tammie also collected rags and the housewife got a 'porridge bowlie' in exchange for the same."

The bakers, grocers and fish merchants visited the farms and cottages originally with horses and carts and then with vans. Johnnie McIntosh drove the van for Andrew Nicol, Fancy Bread and Biscuit Baker. Jessie MacPherson remembered that a 4lb loaf cost 4d and that it was a great treat to get one of his caraway seed loaves. There was also the Brewery Cart. These carts went off the road at the end of the 19th century and were known for their smart horses and attractive turn out.

There was also "Breid Rabbie" who used to walk as far as Udny selling her bread and rowies, a remarkable achievement considering how large she was. And in the 1940s "Greetin Johnnie" came from Boddom to sell fish.

Sadly, most of the shops have disappeared and been converted into private houses. Only the Post Office, The Mace, the Hairdresser "Ythan Waves" and the Butcher's Shop, Reid Brothers remain.

Master Sangster in fancy dress 1930s.   Photograph courtesy of Hazel Stuart.

Alexander and Margaret Sangster.   Photograph courtesy of Hazel Stuart.

The Sangsters relaxing on the Ythan.   Photograph courtesy of Hazel Stuart.

Margaret Sangster.   Photograph courtesy of Hazel Stuart.

The Fisherfolk houses which used to be on Main Street.   Photo courtesy of Bob Stewart.

The Police Station circa 1910.

Main Street looking south circa 1920.   Photograph courtesy of Bob Stewart.

The Foveran Burn in Newburgh circa 1920. Photograph courtesy of Dick Fleming.

Professor George Dunnet with a fulmar.   Photograph courtesy of Culterty Field Station.

Colin Young ringing eider.   Photograph courtesy of Culterty Field Station.

Culterty is an ecological Field Station belonging to Aberdeen University's Department of Zoology. Although research is carried out into animal and plant life throughout Scotland, the centre specialises in the ecology of the Ythan estuary and Forvie National Nature Reserve, making the Ythan the most studied and fully understood estuary in Britain. Culterty also trains undergraduate and post-graduate students in environmental sciences.

Under Professor Dunnet and his successors, the Field Station is now recognised all over the world as a centre of expertise in animal populations, their food and feeding and social organisation. Scientists study single species such as the eider and also the food web - who eats who out there on the estuary.

It was Professor Wynne-Edwards in the 1950s who saw the potential of Culterty and persuaded Aberdeen University to buy it. The Field Station opened its doors in 1958 with George Dunnet in charge and Sandy Anderson as research assistant.

Culterty very quickly gained an international reputation as a centre of excellence for ecological studies and research students began to arrive not only from Britain, but from Iceland, Canada, the Far East, Africa, Australia and the States. A great many Culterty graduates are now in high positions as academics and politicians all over the world.

Culterty 1980s showing the ornamental ponds.   Photograph courtesy of Culterty Field Station.

Netting swans for ringing.   Photograph courtesy of Culterty Field Station.

Colin Young, pictured ringing eider duck, quite literally got off the bus in Newburgh and three years later left with a Ph.D.

The impact on Newburgh of the students from abroad was enormous. Many of them lived either in rented houses or in digs and took part in village life. There was Joe from Malaysia, for example, who was president of the Badminton Club and everyone knew when Barathi, his Indian wife, was cooking because the exotic smell of her curries wafted down Main Street.

Their children went to Newburgh Mathers or to Slains School and learned to speak English with a broad Buchan accent. Miss Craigmyle, the infant teacher in Newburgh, nearly despaired of one little Israeli girl, Sigalith Yon-Tov, who said nothing at all for a whole term. Suddenly the penny dropped however, and Sigalith never looked back.

Both the staff at Culterty and people in the village were somewhat surprised when one Sudanese student announced that his proxy bride was about to arrive. A year later, their pale coloured baby attracted a great deal of interest and admiration.

Although originally from Duns on the Borders of Scotland rather than further afield, many people still remember Billy Murray with affection. Known locally as the Bird Man of Newburgh, he worked as a technician at Culterty for over 20 years and took an active part in many of the research projects at the Field Station.

During the winter, Billy gave lectures in the surrounding villages on the bird life of Britain. His great passion was ornithology and he was the first person to identify the collared dove in Scotland.

Behind Culterty is the world's first purpose-built ocean Lander research laboratory. Landers, or robot vehicles, enable scientists to study animals and other forms of life living at depths of up to 6000 meters. It is not possible to study such creatures out of their own environment as they are killed by changes in pressure and temperature when captured.

There are large steel tanks, environment chambers and pressure vessels at Oceanlab in which scientists can simulate high pressure conditions and test cameras, sonar equipment and materials used to build the robots. Landers are dropped on to the sea bed and remain there for up to a year transmitting and collecting data.

The exterior is Western Red Cedar and among the energy saving features is a turf roof seeded with stonecrop plants which provides excellent insulation. The entrance and stairs have decks and handrails as in a ship to reflect Oceanlab's maritime function. The building is very environmentally friendly. It is also both functional and attractive and has won several prestigious awards.

Oceanlab.

Little Billy. The Bird Man of Newburgh.

M.Sc. students on a field trip. Photos courtesy of Culterty Field Station.

Sandy Anderson (right) measuring the length of a fulmar's beak.

"Newburgh is distant about 13 miles from Aberdeen by road due north – no train. The people are of the fishing order. The fish – speldings and yellow – are considered famous. The salmon fishing is good and the Ythan is a capital river for the rod. The sea trout are very nice and anyone who desires can get a good days sport here. The inhabitants are very proud of their village."
Notes by William Fiddes Smith.

Holyrood Chapel. The site of the original school.   Photograph courtesy of Christine Fordyce.

Pupils at Newburgh Mathers with headmaster Peter Anton 1890s.   Photograph Dick Fleming.

Until 1872 when the Education Act (Scotland) created parish School Boards and made them legally responsible for providing education for all children between the ages of 5 and 13, Newburgh Mathers was controlled by the magistrates of Aberdeen using money from the Mathers bequest.

John Mathers, the son of Robert Mathers from Mill of Newburgh, made his considerable fortune as a surveyor in India. He left £4000 from the interest of which he directed £55 a year to be paid for educating and clothing 20 children of poor fishermen so that they might become "indentured apprentices for the sea". Navigation was a compulsory subject and, according to Jessie McPherson, there was a mast with rigging in the school grounds on which the boys could learn their future trade.

John Mathers also left £5 a year for three years to enable poor but able pupils to buy books and prepare themselves for college.

The early schoolteachers must have been very dedicated as they sent students direct to University, a rare achievement in those days. Isobella Burgess, who taught at Newburgh Mathers, was one of the family whose name is given to the cottages to the north of Newburgh House. Among the first women graduates of Aberdeen University, she was awarded the degree of L.L.A., the original ladies' equivalent of the M.A.

One of the first tasks of the new Foveran Parish School Board, made up of owners and occupiers of property valued at £4 or more, was to provide another building as the existing one was far too small for the large number of pupils. In the 1870s, the school was in the building which is now Holyrood Chapel on Main Street.

Newburgh Mathers circa 1910. The roof of the Toll House can be seen in the background.

Photograph courtesy of Bob Stewart.

1906 Headmaster Mr Williams.   Photograph courtesy of Bob Stewart.

A new Newburgh Mathers School was planned and built on the Toll Road (School Road today) and in 1882 it opened its doors with Peter Anton as headmaster.

In the late 1880s, the school regime was very strict. Pupils were taught arithmetic, grammar, geography and dictation but, worst of all, were required to know the Second Catechism off by heart. The teacher, pointer in one hand and tawse in the other, would carry out rigorous oral examinations of the children's ability to answer all 107 questions. Local ministers came at regular intervals to test the pupils in Religious Knowledge.

The Mathers bequest of £5 a year for three years was awarded to the painter and etcher James McBey, much to the surprise of his teacher. He spent 7/6d (35p) of it on his first set of oil paints.

The Education Act of 1901 raised the school leaving age to 14 and the school became a Junior Secondary.

In 1903, when William Williams was head teacher, the only water was from a well in the street. This lack of an adequate supply of water for both lavatories and for drinking purposes was pointed out to the School Board by the Inspector.

During the first half of the 20th century, there were regular outbreaks of flu, diphtheria, scarlet fever, German measles, mumps, chicken pox and whooping cough. In 1928 Mr Youngson wrote, "Attendance very poor. Flu prevalent and there are several children suffering from severe illness - Sam Stewart TB. Alex Youngson has been absent for months following rheumatic fever." And in 1938, Mr Lyall reported, "There are twenty-five

1916 Headmaster Mr William Williams.   Photograph courtesy of Ian Stephen.

Newburgh Mathers 1938.   Photograph courtesy of Bob Stewart.

children absent with measles, 10 contacts and five cases of mumps. There are only 64 children present today."

In September 1904, the Compulsory Officer visited the school and took note of the names of several pupils who had not returned after the summer holidays.

An interesting entry by Mr Williams in his log book in January 1909 reads:

"Particulars ascertained from scholars regarding milk used as an article of diet. Scholars present 160 - 6 do not partake of milk food: 154 partake of milk food once or oftener daily, 66 twice daily."

On the 20th of May 1910 the school was closed to observe a day of national mourning following the death of Edward V11 and an extra week of holiday was given in June at the command of King George V who was crowned on the 22nd of that month.

Mr Williams noted that on December 13th 1912 attendance had been good apart from the Tuesday of that week when 16 boys were beating at a hunt.

All the senior girls were allowed to attend cookery classes on February 22nd 1918 to learn war cookery recipes. The girls had also begun war-work knitting during the Industrial Work period.

In January 1923, Mr R. W. Youngson took over as headmaster. During his tenure, he was often permitted leave to continue his Territorial Army Training.

Newburgh Mathers 1971.   Photograph courtesy of Sandy MacDonald.

Newburgh Mathers Primary 7 1980.   Photograph courtesy of Ian Stephen.

A wireless was installed for a day in April 1924 to allow the pupils to hear the speeches of H.M. King George and the Prince of Wales at Wembley.

In March 1925, the engineer at Waterside Bridge visited the school to say that no children from the far side of the river would be permitted to cross the bridge while the new bridge was being built. In May, these children were removed from the register and sent to Slains School.

Mr Youngson reported in September 1930 that "the morning was very wet and many of the country children arrived soaked. Put on fires and dried them as best we could."

In March 1935 Mr Andrew Lyall became headmaster. It was the silver Jubilee of George V in May of that year and all the children were presented with a commemorative medal. A few days later, after going to church in the morning, the pupils enjoyed a Jubilee party on the links where they were entertained by a conjurer.

Efforts were being made by the County Medical Service to eliminate diphtheria and at the end of October 1935, 51 children were tested under the Diphtheria Immunisation Scheme.

Later that year, Mr Lyall wrote in the school log book, "The condition of the playground is causing me some concern. Some of the infants are abusing it instead of going to the lavatories. I have again warned all children against this practice."

There is little mention of the war in the log book until 1940 when Mr Lyall records that on June 10th of that year he and Constable Gilmour examined the children's respirators (gas masks) and replaced the ones that had become too small.

Photograph courtesy of Pam Ritchie & Ian Stephen.

In 1985 Primary 3 at Newburgh Mathers nominated their Lollipop Lady, Mrs Wendy Jones for the Press and Journal Lollipop Person of the Year Competition. The class submitted a folder of pictures and articles to explain why they thought she should win. They said that as well as performing her 'lollipop' duties, Mrs Jones tied shoelaces, chased dogs from the playground, gave all the children a lollipop at the end of term and told car drivers not to park in the wrong place.

Back left to right: Nicola Smith, Ewan McAndrew, James Fairclough, Alan Cooper, Darren Glennie, Gavin Slessop, Andrew Marshall, Ian Adams, Adam McBain, Stuart Tennant, Neil Strachan, Gayle Ritchie, Sarah Heath.

Front left to right: Claire Brankin, Christine Gray, Karen Murray, Gillian Penny, Dana White, Mrs Wendy Jones, Gayle Beveridge, Nicola Jamieson.

By October 1940, air raids over Aberdeen were becoming more frequent and air raid warnings were interrupting everyday life. Pupils were late for school if the siren had sounded during the night and lessons were abandoned when it went off during school hours. By February of 1941 however, when the siren sounded at 10.15 a.m., the children remained in the classroom. The Director of Education had approved a spotter system and work was to carry on if there were no aircraft in the vicinity.

On January 29th 1942, the school was closed in the afternoon for the funerals of James Walker and George Whyte, the two lifeboat men who were drowned as the lifeboat was coming back into the estuary.

The District Nurse paid a visit on September 18th as there had been reports that some children were infested with vermin and scabies.

In May 1944, William Innes and Ed Aiken were given temporary exemption from school to plant potatoes at Knockhall Farm. When they didn't reappear, Mr Lyall set out to find them. They had finished planting the potatoes but the farmer had asked them to do other work. The boys were sent back to school and the farmer warned not to do that again.

In 1955, there were 105 pupils with four full-time teachers and four visiting teachers. In 1964, when Newburgh Mathers became a Primary School rather than a Junior Secondary, the roll fell to 70. By 1973 there were only 45 pupils and two teachers. During the late 1970s and 1980s however, as oil-related families began to move into the village, there was a marked increase in pupil numbers. By 1987, the roll was 158 with seven full-time teachers, and by 1989, it was 170.

More pupils needed more space so in 1980 and again in 1984, when Mrs Margaret Galloway was head teacher, the original school building was extended.

In 1982, to celebrate the School's centenary and the first part of the new extension, pupils in Primary 7 decided to bury a time capsule under the

Art teacher David Cordiner recording the pupils of Primary 7 before the time capsule was buried.

1999 with head teacher Mr Ian Stephen.

building. They went round the other classes explaining what they were doing and asking for suggestions and contributions. When the lid was sealed down, the capsule contained information about the school and the village, details of the pupils, their teachers, classwork, favourite sweets and television programmes.

In 1987, when Mrs Galloway was still head teacher, the school was given a glowing report by H.M. Inspectors of Schools with headlines in the press reading, "Top Marks to Newburgh Mathers." This tradition of excellence continued with Mr Ian Stephen in charge. In 2004, the Inspectors wrote, "Aberdeenshire Council wishes to congratulate the Head Teacher and staff at Newburgh Mathers on the strengths identified."

Newburgh Mathers
Football Team 2004.

The new extension.

54

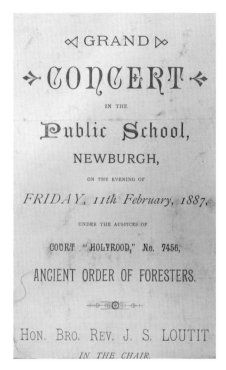

During the 1880s, the highlight of the winter was The Foresters' Concert held in the School. The Ancient Order of Foresters was a mutual insurance club providing benefits in cases of injury and sickness or to dependants on the death of a member. By the end of the 19th century, almost every town and village had at least one such society.

Most of the artists in the Grand Concert were from Foveran parish with Dove Paterson from Aberdeen as the star turn. He may well have been persuaded to come to Newburgh by his sister who was married to Johnnie McIntosh, van man to Andrew Nicol, baker in the village. Dove Paterson's speciality was humorous recitations such as 'Touch me gin ye daur' or 'The Funnygraph'. Amongst his other accomplishments, Dove Paterson was one of the first people in the North East to talk on cine film.

He also presented an Acetylene Lighting Plant to Holyrood Chapel and donated the seat on the Links known as The Dove's Rest. Unfortunately, the seat no longer exists. Newburgh Youth Club's efforts to find it in the 1990s were unsuccessful.

Ancient Order of Foresters. Concert Programme.

Part First: Chairman's Address.

Duet: (piano and violin)		Mrs Anderson & Mrs Ritchie
Duet:	'Very Suspicious'	Misses Menzies
Recitation:	'Flat Contradiction'	Mr Ross
Song Comic	'Brown'	Mr J. W. Davidson
Recitation: Humorous	'To a Scotch Haggis'	Mr Dove Paterson
Duet: (piano and violin)		Miss Easton & Mr Smith
Song:	'At the Ferry'	Mrs Anderson
Recitation: Pathetic	'Papa's Letter'	Mr Dove Paterson
Song:	'The Bonnie Banks o' Loch Lomond'	Miss Coutts
Trio:	'He's owre the Hills'	Mrs Buchan, Mr J. Rae & Mr J. A. Williamson
Song: Comic	'The Parcels Post'	Mr J. W. Davidson

Part Second.

Duet: (piano and violin)		Miss Easton & Mr Smith
Song:	'Jessie's Dream'	Mrs Anderson
Recitation: Humorous	'Willie Wastle's Courtship'	Mr Dove Paterson
Song:	'Shells of the Ocean'	Mr Ross
Song: Comic	'McAllistair's Bonnet'	Mr J. W. Davidson
Duet: (piano and violin)		Mrs Anderson & Mrs Ritchie
Trio:	'There was a Lad'	Mrs Buchan, Mr J. A. Rae & Mr J. W. Williamson
Duet:	'Down the Burn Davie'	Misses Menzies
Recitation: Humorous	'Jud Brownin's Account of Rubenstein's Playing'	Mr Dove Paterson

George Ross with his bus in Mealmarket Street in Aberdeen 1920s.
Photograph courtesy of Alex Ross.

During the latter part of the 19th century, the horse bus station in Newburgh was owned by the McBey family. They sold the business to George Cruickshank around the turn of the 20th century. With so many horses to feed, George bought the farm Ythan Lodge in 1906 but by the early 1920s, motorised transport had arrived and the need for horses declined. In 1919, after consulting with his sons, he decided to sell the farm and concentrate on transport rather than farming.

George Cruickshank gradually motorised his horse drawn vehicles by bolting both his horse drawn bus, and his horse drawn hearse onto Ford lorry chassis. When he first used the new hearse, someone complimented him on the splendid reconstruction.

"Folk are fair dyin' to get the use o' it," said George. He also supplied taxis and all the cars for local funerals.

In the 1920s, George Ross, George Cruickshank's nephew, was running the Newburgh bus service in competition with The Railway Bus. (The Railway Bus was 4/- return to Newburgh while George charged 2/- return.)

After George Cruickshank died in 1931, his business was divided into two sections. His son Alexander and nephew George joined forces to form Cruickshank & Ross. They ran the bus side of the business while another son John ran the haulage side. As well as the bus service based in Newburgh, there was also a service based in Fyvie,

For many years, Cruickshank & Ross and Mitchell & Rae were the main employers in Newburgh. Ian Cruickshank, John's son, took over the haulage business.

DISPLENISH SALE
OF HIRER'S PLANT AND FARM
IMPLEMENTS,
At YTHAN LODGE, NEWBURGH.
On SATURDAY, 3rd MAY.

The Subscribers, favoured with instructions from Mr George Cruickshank, will Sell, by Public Auction, the undernoted—

LIVE STOCK.

4 Strong WORK HORSES and MARES, 6 to 10 years old, suitable for Cart and Lorry Work.
8 Superior DAIRY COWS in good season.
3 Strong HEIFERS, in Calf.
Black Polled BULL, 2 years old, grand server.
10 Two-year-old BULLOCKS and HEIFERS, mostly Black Polled and nearly fat.
8 Yearling BULLOCKS and HEIFERS, extra good.
6 Young CALVES.

IMPLEMENTS.—4 Box Carts, two with Tops; 2 Lorries, Double or Single (almost new); Rubber-tyred Landau, very light; Brougham, 'Bus (light), suitable for station work; Brake, seated for ten; Light Waggonette, and few Sleighs, Ralli Car, Cattle Float, almost new; Funeral Car in first-class order; Char-a-Banc, seated for thirty; Single-Seated Baker's Gig, Spring Cart, Single D.F. (special), D.B., and Water Fur Ploughs; Potato, 2 Sets Iron, and Chain Harrows; Shim and Cultivator combined, 3-horse Grub-

ber, Manure Distributor, Dung-breaker, Massey-Harris and Hornsby Binders, Albion Mower, Broadcast Sowing Machine, Horse Rake, Hay Gatherer, Turnip Sowing Machine, Turnip Puller, Metal and Stone Rollers, Box Barrows, Cake Breaker (good as new), Potato Digger, Bogey for Harrows, Ladders, Hand Hurley, etc., etc.

BARN FURNITURE AND HARNESS.—Steelyard and Weights, Barn Fan, by Baker; Coir Yarn, Forks, Yokes, Swingletrees, Cart Girdings, Brushes, Combs, etc.; Clippers for Sheep and Horses; set of Single and Double Harness, 3 Sets Cart and Plough Harness, in first-class condition; Set Harness for Double Lorry, several Lots of Odd Harness, Harness Stool, and the usual Stable Furnishings. Four to Six Bar-Hives and Bees, with all Apiary Accessories. Tamlin's Incubator, almost new.

FURNITURE.—Organ, Round Mahogany Centre Table, Couch in Plush, Couch, Couch in Leather, Marble-Topped Table, 9 H.B. Chairs, Window Table, Brussels Carpet, 15 by 18; Carpet, 12 by 12; Draught Screen, Yellow Pine Bedroom Suite of 5 Pieces, 2 Iron Bedsteads, Brass Fender and Fire-irons, Coal Vase, Knife Cleaner, and various other sundry Articles.

Sale to Commence at 9 a.m. with Harness and Minor Implements, Cattle about 2 p.m., followed by Horses and Furniture thereafter.

Mrs Cassie, The Buffet, Ellon, will supply Refreshments at Moderate Charges.

CENTRAL AUCTION MART CO., LTD.,
Auctioneers.

Shall be glad to see you present.

Front left: beside the Model T Ford is John Cruickshank. Centre: William Keith from the shop "Keith's Corner" across the road. Beside the French Sedan is George Cruickshank Snr.

Back: to the left of the Albion Bus is the driver Alec Morrison. Holding the child (Gladys) is her father George W. Cruickshank. With them is George Ross.

Photograph courtesy of Ian Cruickshank

The Garage.   Photographs courtesy of Alex Ross.

The three men are: L-R John Cruickshank, Alex Cruickshank, George Ross.

The driver is Sandy Blackhall. George Cruickshank is standing at the side of the bus.
Photo Dick Fleming.

The Newburgh Bus by William Fiddes Smith 1885.
"Double fare between Aberdeen and the 'fashionable watering place'
Newburgh, NB. Pigs also taken at the same rate."

Sandy Blackhall was born in the parish in 1839 and lived alone in a house by the Spalding Bridge. The house no longer exists. He drove the horse bus between Aberdeen and Newburgh for more than 50 years, first for the McBey family and then for George Cruickshank. The Newburgh Bus was taken off the road around 1900 and replaced by the G.N.S.R. motor bus which was superseded by Cruickshank's bus.

When he was driving, Sandy always wore a lugged bonnet and heavy army coat and it was said he ate breakfast the night before in order to be on time in the morning. He had only one tooth in the front and it was quite a sight to see him chewing on dulse, a kind of seaweed.

He is buried in Holyrood Cemetery and there is a horse carved on his gravestone.

McBey's Stables by William Fiddes Smith 1885.

The Mail Omnibus. Newburgh.   Photograph courtesy of Bob Stewart.

The SA311 was a Milnes-Daimler 20-25HP bus chassis owned and built by the Great North of Scotland Railway. There were 10 upper deck and 10 lower deck seats and another two open air seats next to the driver. The vehicle was owned by G.N.S.R. and then L.N.E.R. from the 13th of April 1907 until March 1926. The buses were a far cry from the luxury coaches of today. They averaged 10 to 12 m.p.h. and their solid rubber tyres combined with the road surfaces of the time must have made for a bone-shaking ride.

The Great North of Scotland Railway operated an Aberdeen - Newburgh bus service from 1st April 1907 until March 1st 1922. It ran from Schoolhill Station (next to HM Theatre) via Bridge of Don, Balmedie and Fontainebleau (sometimes via Foveran) to Newburgh. The G.N.S.R. also ran a steam lorry service between Guild Street goods station to Newburgh around the same time. Early vehicles on the Newburgh run included German-manufactured Durkopps for which G.N.S.R. built their own demountable bodies but these were soon replaced by two Miles-Daimlers which continued in use for many years.

GNSR OMNIBUS SERVICES
Aberdeen and Newburgh. 1907-1922

FARE STAGE	MILEAGE
Aberdeen	0
Aberdeen (County Hotel)	
(Later in GNSR days given as 164 King Street.)	-
Bridge of Don (Post Office)	2¾
Denmore	4
Blackdog (Belhevie)	5¾
Millden	7¼
Balmedie (Post Office)	8
Belhelvie (Post Office)	8½
Aikenshill Road	10½
United Free Church	11¼
Fontainbleau	13¼
Newburgh	14¾

SA 614. The G.N.S.R. Aberdeen and Newburgh Bus.   Photograph courtesy of Buchan Heritage

The Iron Bridge.   Photograph courtesy of Bob Stewart.

The Middle or New Bridge.   Photograph courtesy of Bob Stewart.

At one time there was a ford and a ferry at Tarty and another crossing point below the Sleeks near Waterside where horses and carts would squelch their way across the mud flats. In bad weather or at high tide these crossing points could not be used and a detour of 8 miles via Ellon was necessary.

A bridge was badly needed so in the late 1860s, a committee was formed locally to raise enough money to build one.

By the time the Iron Bridge was opened on July 1877, most of the £4,000 needed had been raised, contributions coming from, amongst others, Lord Aberdeen, Mr Gordon of Cluny and the County Board Trustees.

The depth of silt on the river bed posed problems for Mr Willet, the engineer who designed the bridge. Timber piles covered in concrete were driven into the river to a depth of 20 feet and iron cross joints at 3ft 6" intervals were attached to the piles. Piers, consisting of groups of four cast-iron pillars, were then placed on top of the piles.

To test the strength of the bridge, Mr Willet loaded each arch with a load of 40 tons, equal to the weight of a traction engine and trailer, then waited for two days to see what happened. There was no movement so the bridge was declared strong enough for all traffic likely to cross it.

Half a mile of new roadway was laid on the approaches to the bridge and Mr Hugh McKay was responsible for landscaping the embankments and sowing them with ryegrass.

The bridge, an attractive construction with iron lattice work on both sides, was 300 feet long with a concrete roadway 14 feet wide. It served

A survey carried out for The Regional Transportation and Roads Committee showed that chloride salts in the seawater had saturated the poor quality porous concrete used to cover the steel reinforcement and caused severe corrosion. The bridge was thought no longer capable of carrying the increased volume of traffic safely.

But the New Bridge was stronger than the engineers had thought and it took more than six weeks to demolish.

Work began on the present bridge in March 1986. Steel pipes of varying lengths (9.5m to 24m) were driven into the ground to provide a foundation on which to construct the bridge itself. Steel girders were brought to the site where they were welded together. A huge mobile crane lifted them into their positions.

It was opened on the 23rd of November 1987.

Demolishing the New or Middle Bridge.   Photographs courtesy of Bob Stewart

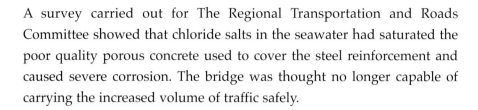

Laying the road surface of the New Bridge   1926.
1926.
Photographs Bob Stewart.

the community until 1926 when it was replaced by the New or Middle Bridge, a much less attractive structure made of concrete.

By the 1980s, the condition of the New Bridge was giving cause for concern as masonry had started to fall off into the river, despite extensive repairs in the 1970s.

The present Waterside Bridge.   Photograph courtesy of Bob Stewart.

61

20-05-86. The digger is trapped in the soft ground.   Photo courtesy of the P&J.

23-03-87. The first steel girders are placed in position.   Photo courtesy of P&J.

24-03-87. Work begins again on the bridge while Mr William Park looks on.   Photo P&J.

26-08-88. Demolishing the old bridge.   Photograph courtesy of the P&J.

Mrs Mabel Aiken at the opening of the new bridge 23-11-87.
Photo courtesy of the P & J.

At the age of 75, Mabel Aiken was the first person to walk across the new bridge at Waterside after the opening ceremony. Several of the construction engineers stayed at "Easties", Mabel's B & B, and they thought it fitting she should be part of the celebrations.

Mabel left school at 14 and began work on a farm at Slains before moving to East Knockhall where she met and married her husband. On the 75 acre farm there were 30 cattle, five milk cows, horses, chickens, calves, ducks and a few pigs to look after.

On a typical day in the 1930s, Mabel would rise at 5am, prepare food for the men, milk the five cows, strain the milk, then feed the chickens. Breakfast was a bowl of milk with oatmeal, salt and pepper and a knob of butter.

Every week the grocer's van arrived to collect 30 dozen eggs and that money paid for the family groceries. She made butter in a hand churn which was sold locally. Cheese she made by heating milk then adding rennet to make it curdle. It was cooled, then broken up and, with salt added, pressed in a cheese press for a few days until the whey disappeared. The cheeses were then placed in the cellar to dry off before being sold.

Dinner was broth twice a week, potato soup, stovies, fried potatoes, rabbit stuffed with oatmeal or dishes made with salt cod, and always oatcakes and home made cheese.

Every Monday the dentist came from Aberdeen to Ellon and, if contacted, would come past the house to extract a tooth. A painful experience, Mabel recalled.

At Foveran School there was a lot of spelling and long dictation and reciting of the catechism. When the minister came every month in his trap to talk to the pupils, the girls had to curtsey and the boys salute.

Mabel walked the two and a half miles there and back every day and on cold wet mornings the children were allowed to stand by the guard to the open fire to dry their socks and stockings. Those who were better off had buttoned boots which were more expensive than the plain lacing ones. In the summer the children often ran barefoot and played skipping games and "beddies".

Butcher's Bridge.

The Spalding Bridge.

The three foot bridges which cross the Foveran Burn are the gateways from the village to the links and the beach.

The Butcher's Bridge is so called because the killing house was nearby. (Jessie McPherson remembered that when a cow was killed by the butcher, a bell was rung to let housewives know meat was available.)

The Spalding Bridge was named after its donor Captain Thomas Spalding of the Aberdeen Star Line which sailed to Australia. At one time, Captain Thomas was on the Themopylae, one of the famous clippers.

The Fisher Briggie could have been named by fishermen heading for the estuary. The water to the left of the Fisher Briggie used to be known as the Hauchie which means low lying ground at the side of a stream. In winter this area used to be flooded and any ice formed on it was collected by the salmon fishers and taken to the Ice House near the Corf House at the end of Beach Road.

There was a fourth bridge at the end of Stephen's Lane but it has long since disappeared.

In 1940, the bridges were in a poor state of repair and for several Saturday nights dances were held in the Public Hall to raise funds for their repair.

In 1979, floods damaged all three bridges, the Spalding Bridge in particular. The estimate for repairs to it was £4000, while the other two were thought to need about £1000 each.

The newly formed Foveran Community Council joined forces with Newburgh Amenities and, with Sandy Anderson as chairman, formed the Bridge Sub-Committee to raise the money.

Among the fund-raising efforts was a cookery demonstration by Mrs Bates from the Udny Arms, a slide shoe by Bob Davis, a concert by the Ythan Singers, a sale of work in the village and a musical evening "Barfit & Broke". Envelopes were delivered to every household and by May 1980, £3,500 had been collected. Contributions could also be handed in at the Newburgh Branch of the Clydesdale Bank.

The Countryside Commission, with a little help from Gordon District Council, undertook to pay for the work on the Butcher's Bridge, but it was the army of volunteers - John Cook, Bob Barclay, Nigel Briggs, Brian Fagg, Jim Massie, George Moir, Alex Smith, Dick Fleming and many more - who did all the repair work to make the bridges useable and safe once again. By the time they had finished, all three bridges were in much better condition than anyone could remember. The final cost was £8,683.

Fisher Briggie.

Kevin Moir and Duncan Farr watch as work begins to repair The Spalding Bridge.   Photo P&J.

June Argo at the old Spalding Bridge 1936.
Photo courtesy of Richard Argo.

The Founding Fathers.   Photograph courtesy of Newburgh Golf Club.

Photograph courtesy of Newburgh Golf Club and Bob Stewart.

Newburgh Golf Club was founded in 1888 and was a nine-hole course measuring 1 mile and 401 yards. The original patron was John H. Udny of Udny who remained as president until 1938.

In his autobiography, James McBey wrote that in the 1890s "Every boy in the village had his lacerated gutta-percha golf ball and his cleek which served him as a driver, iron, mashie, putter and general weapon….. The golf flags marking the holes on the Links were tall bars of half-inch square iron with two circles of sheet iron riveted at right angles to the top end."

In September 1912, an eighteen-hole course was opened on the same area of ground but reverted to being a nine-hole course after World War 1.

In the early 1920s, the Golf Club was known as the Golf and Tennis Club. At that time the courts were on the edge of the golf course in front of the pavilion. In 1922 the membership was 128 and the Club joined the North East District Association of the Scottish Golf Union. Until the outbreak of World War 11, it was well patronised.

In 1947, the Club was reborn and nine holes were played until 1994 when land to the south of the old course on the Links was bought. With the help of Greens of Scotland who designed the new nine holes, Lottery funding and a great deal of hard work by Club members, the extended par 72 course was opened in 1996.

Since then, a new clubhouse, designed by David Warrender, has been built. It was opened on the 13th of April 2001 by Open Champion Paul Lawrie in the presence of sponsors and members.

Funding for the £675,000 facility came from sportscotland Lottery Fund,

The opening of the Golf and Tennis Club.
Photograph courtesy of Bob Stewart.

Alan MacDonald on the Links 1940s.
Photo Sandy MacDonald.

Aberdeenshire Council and the Belhelvie and Foveran Community Trust.

The construction of the extra nine holes on the golf course necessitated the removal of the water header tank which stood behind where the new clubhouse now is. Did the Golf Club realise that they had taken away Newburgh's own fertility clinic? It seems that if a young woman sat under the tank when the moon was in a certain place, the chances of her conceiving were greatly enhanced.

The day out described in this letter to a local newspaper must have happened before 1924 as "The Despatch" went out of service that year.

"Golfers Who Flew the White Ensign".

"Sir,

I wonder what the Lord King of Arms would have thought of an incident that happened in Newburgh about sixty years ago. The Peterhead Golf Club and the Newburgh Golf Club arranged for a match to be played at Peterhead.

The Newburgh Golf Club planned to go to Peterhead by sea. They got the steam tug the 'Despatch' (crew: - Captain William Reid, Engineer: - Mr James Duguid) to take them round.

The village joiner, George Ross, who kept everything from a needle to an anchor, looked out a flag for them from a bunch of flags. The one he gave them was The White Ensign - reserved for ships of the Royal Navy or the Royal Yacht Squadron. The coastguards at Collieston picked it out and signalled to the Peterhead coastguards.

On arrival in Peterhead, the golfers were challenged, but by that time, the majority of the golfers were so seasick that their only desire was to reach dry land. It might have been the Jolly Roger for all they cared. I'm afraid there wasn't much golf played. They got home but not with the White Ensign flying.

No more was heard of the matter from any authority. It was taken all in good part, but the golfers were warned: 'Don't do it again!'

Signed 'Not A Golfer.'"

Alistair Sinclair (Captain) and Paul Lawrie at the opening of the new club house 13th April 2001. Photo P & J.

The new clubhouse resembles the shape of the arctic tern which is the Club emblem.

The opening ceremony. L-R Captain Alistair Sinclair with sportscotland respresentative and Paul Lawrie. Photograph courtesy of the P & J.

John H. Udny of Udny, the original patron of the Golf Club. Photo courtesy of Newburgh Golf Club.

Newburgh Football Club was first formed over 100 years ago but no one is quite sure of the date as few records were kept.

One account from the 1920s does reveal that the Club made an appearance at Pittodrie, the score being 5-0 in favour of Aberdeen.

In 1926-27, the Club was in the Central Buchan League when Ellon won the Hepburn Cup with Newburgh as runners up. In the final, the score was 5-5 but as Ellon had played more matches, they took the trophy - and the referee was escorted from the pitch by the local policeman.

Between the wars, the "friendlies" were eagerly anticipated, one in particular being the annual visit of the Barbers, a team sponsored by Mr Bain, a hairdresser from Aberdeen. Among the players to come to Newburgh for those matches were Scottish International inside forwards Bobby Bruce, Jock Hutton and Paddy Travers.

In the programme (shown left) for the 1951 Festival of Sport, there are notes on the players in the football team.

THURLOW FRASER: 'a quiet unassuming type of person'
GEORGE THOM: 'has distinguished himself as goalkeeper'
ALEX ELDER: 'popularly known as 'Trenchie', a real asset'
ALBERT SORRIE: 'no keener player, realises his limitations but does his best'
GORDON COPLAND: 'crisp, keen kicker and keen tackler'
WILLIAM WOOD: 'popularly known as 'Skallie', a real find'
DOUGLAS GRAY: 'has a good head and right foot, but learn to use the other one!'
GEORGE SHEWAN: 'best ball player in the team, must shed weight'
GEORGE CRUICKSHANK: 'speedy winger with strong right foot'
DONALD WOOD: 'Donlie can work the ball but inclined to hang on too long'
GEORGE MORRISON: 'powerfully built, must improve timing with head'
JOHN DUFFUS: 'plenty of dash, temperamental'

1926-7 (back) Jimmy Rae, Hebbie Gall, Bill Walker, Basil Leslie, Shy Duncan, Edwin Beverley, John Cruickshank. (front) Bill Hutcheon, Mr Samuel, William Wood, Jim Arthur, James Stewart, James Walker.

PROGRAMME

MONDAY
Fancy Dress Football Match
Over 35s v Under 25s, commencing 7.30 p.m.
100 yards handicap race will be run during the interval.

TUESDAY
Children's Sports

WEDNESDAY
Central Buchan League Football Match at 8 p.m.
Newburgh v Maud

THURSDAY
Five - a - side Football Tournament

FRIDAY
At 7.39 p.m. Music by OLD

MELDRUM PIPE BAND
At 8 p.m. Football Match. NEWBURGH Select v ELLON Select.
At 9 p.m. **DANCING** in Public Hall to music by BILLY MENNIE and His All-Star Band.
At 10.15 p.m. **CROWNING OF THE FESTIVAL QUEEN**.

SATURDAY
At 6 p.m. MUSIC in the Square by STONEYWOOD WORKS SILVER BAND.
At 6.30 p.m. Football Match—**Newburgh v. Fisherford**.
At 8 p.m. In Public Hall
Exhibition
by HEALTH and STRENGTH SOCIETY and ABERDEEN SPARTAN CLUB
2 Challenge Free-Style Wrestling Matches
Display of Gymnastics
Strand Pulling Contest
by well-known record holders
Arranged through the courtesy of Mr IAN SMITH, President, Aberdeen Health and Strength Club.
At 8.45 p.m.
DANCE
to Music by the Melodair's Dance Band

GOD SAVE THE KING

Mrs Innes at the corf house. Mrs Innes is Pearl Elrick's great grandmother. Early 1900s.
Photo courtesy of Pearl Elrick.

Ma great-granfaither wis cockswain o the Neebora life boat, an ma grandfaither wis the skipper. They baith got medals frae the Queen fur life-savin.

This wis the wye o't. Awa back in the 1920s, at the heicht o a storm, wird cam that a boatie wis sinkin. Weemin in thon days got sixpence fur helping tae launch the life boat, sae fin the syreen went, a' the weemin ran tae get the sixpence. The first eens there was gien a sash tae weir, tae show that they war the pullers. Anely the weemin weirin the sash got tae pull oot the lifeboat an earn the sixpence. Weel, they launched the life boat, an the sea wis really roch an coorse… great muckle waves. Fin ma granfaither reached the boat, it wis hauf aneth the watter, an fowk was haudin ontae the mast, bit he managed tae save them, an they war gey gled tae see him!

Durin the war, ma grandfaither, Jimmy Innes, wis coast guard. He'd tae wauk richt across the beach an ging intae a hoosie tae watch the coast, fur fear o ony German boats tryin tae lan. He wis nicht watchman. He waukit oot across the san fin it wis dairk, bit there wis a phone there in the hoosie sae he didna feel ower cut aff.

Fin I wis a littlin, I gaed wi ma grannie doon tae the shoppie, bit it tuik an affa lang time because she spoke tae aabody. We gaed tae the burn an guddlit fur bandies. It wis fine an sunny, an grannie bocht a bag o broken biscuits an a bottle o lemonade. We a' got a sook ooto the bottle. I mind it tastit sanny… bits o san got intae the ale fae the beach, far we'd set the bottle doon fin we war haein wir picnic. Whiles she made sugar-allie watter. She bocht hard liquorice fae the chemist, pit it inno a bottle fu o plain watter an shook it up an doon. It wis a sweet drink.

I eesed tae gaither wild flooers fin I wis a bairn, an press them, an ma grannie learned me foo tae makk hats an rattles fae the rashes that grew in Joseph's pond doon aside the salmon fishie's hoose. The hats lookit like wigwams…it wis jist the bairns that wore them. Fin we pued the rashes they war fite at the fit, an saft. We sookit the fit o them… the rashes were tasted like bamboo.

Some o's cam ower tae Collieston an collecktit gulls eggs, or gaed ower tae Slains Castle fur mushrooms fin they war in season.

We gaithered thyme aff the links tae pit aneth oor pillas tae makk us sleep. An aabody cam oot tae Forvie an gaithered annets' eggs an cured them wi watter glaiss. Ye bocht yon fae the chemist. It sealed the raw eggs, sae they didna ging wrang. Ma grannie used them fin she wis bakin. The eggs war left in the watter glaiss a' the time.

Jimmy Innes by James McBey. Jimmy Innes was coxswain of the lifeboat from 1908 -1931.
He was Pearl Elrick's grandfather.   Photograph courtesy of Aberdeen Art Gallery.

A mannie eence gaed ma mither intae a row fur disturbin the annets, bit ma mither telt him that lang ago we aye pickit the first clutch o eggs an the annets laid mair. Ma mither eased tae tak the fluff aff their nests an pit it inside pillacases. Syne she'd drap them intae the byler an byle them. They's come up a' fine an fluffy an clean efter they'd bin byled an dried. Fowk made quilts ooto them, bit we aye used the feathers fur pillas.

Ma grandfaither wis a salmon fisher. He netted the salmon in the Ythan, an durin the fishin season he bede in a bothie there. Ma great granny bede in thon bothie a' simmer, an she crived aff a wee plot an grew carrots in the san. There's nae wirms in san that ett the carrots like there is among yird. Ma fowk keepit hens an turkies there ana.

We gathered dulse frae Collieston, an efter we'd gathered it, we tuik it hame an reid-hetted it on the fire, tae gar it dry oot. It tasted fine an crunchy syne. Sometimes we got tangles frae Collieston.. Tangles are lang, broony-green in colour. Ye fin them aside the dulse. A man ca'd John Sutherland wad cairry a big bunnie o tangles back tae Neebra, an we jist ett them raw. They're affa guid fur ye - fu o iron!

Pearl Elrick

The Udny Arms established its reputation as a haven for fishermen well over a hundred years ago, but whether the two princes from Siam who stayed there for the month of July in 1898 were fishermen, is not known. James Robertson Justice certainly was and during the late 1930s he enjoyed fishing for both salmon and sea trout. As was the custom, he would weigh his catch on the scales in the hotel entrance and record it in the Fishing Book.

Mr John Ritchie was proprietor for nearly forty four years from the 1880s until the 1920s. He was clearly an effective fund raiser as he was responsible for raising enough money to set up the Golf Club and build the Public Hall. His other contributions to village life included being on the Parish Council, the Ellon District Committee and he was Chairman of the Lifeboat Committee.

Pearl Elrick's father George started work in the hotel at the age of 14 and remained there for 12 years. John Ritchie had an original way of making George save. He banked all George's wages for him and would only allow him to keep his tips as pocket money.

From 1965-73, the Udny Arms was owned by Dr Wilfred Bates and it was his wife Renee who established the hotel's reputation for fine food.

Keith Schellenberg of Udny & Dudwick Estates took over in 1973 then sold it again in 1976. The hotel was advertised as being "perfectly placed to take all possible advantage of the most prosperous and economically secure area in the country." It was the early days of North Sea oil.

During the 1980s when Walter McInlay and his wife Veronica were the owners, the hotel became known throughout Scotland as a centre for the game of petanque, a version of bowls. Played on pitches built into the car park, it was taken very seriously and in May 1982 around 70 teams from all over the country competed in the Scottish Petanque Championships. The highly competitive sessions were usually followed by ceilidhs in the evening.

The present owners, the Craig family from Glasgow, took over in 1986 and have succeeded in maintaining the hotel's relaxed and friendly atmosphere. Petanque may no langer be played but people still come to fish, walk on Forvie, play golf or listen to the eiders gossiping on the estuary.

Newburgh 1952.

Photograph courtesy of P&J.

Briggies in the 1880s by William Fiddes Smith.

Briggies 1950s. Photograph courtesy of Carolyn Smith.

There has been an inn at the bridge for longer than anyone can remember.

The picture above dating from the 1880s is by Wiliam Fiddes Smith, fiddle player and faithful patron of the establishment. The house with the little gothic window on the left of the main building used to be known as "The Caravan" and the larger house on the right was at one time the baker's shop and then a dwelling house and shop. Both were demolished before the turn of the 20th century.

In the background with a flag on top is the Gallow Hill where Helene Fraser from Aikenshill was burned as a witch at the stake in 1597 after the Foveran Presbytery found her guilty of 14 charges of "publict and commond charming".

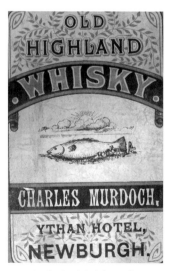

A whisky label from the late 19th century.

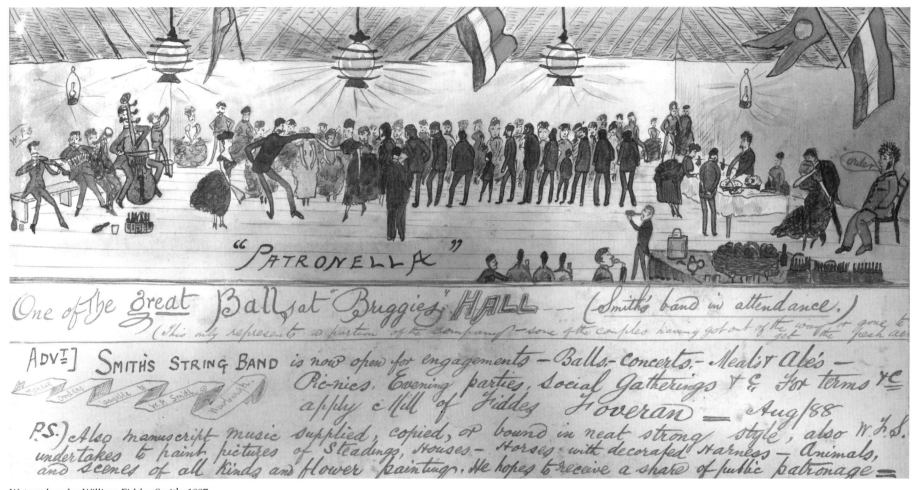

Watercolour by William Fiddes Smith. 1887

"PATRONELLA"
"One of the great Balls at "Briggies" HALL-(Smith's band in attendance.)
(This only represents a portion of the company - some of the couples having got out of the way and gone to get the fresh ale)
ADVT. SMITH'S STRING BAND is now open for engagements - Balls - Concerts - Meals & Ales - Pic-nics, Evening parties, Social Gatherings
For terms Apply Mill of Fiddes, Foveran - Aug/88
PS) Also manuscript music supplied, copied or bound in neat strong style, also W.F.S. undertakes to paint pictures
of Steadings, Houses - Horses with decorated harness - Animals and scenes of all kinds and flower paintings.
He hopes to receive a share of public patronage." by William Fiddes Smith 1885.

"SATURDAY EVENING ENTERTAINMENTS at Newburgh = Ythan Hotel (Briggies)
The fun goes fast and furious here on Saturday nights and "special" nights." by William Fiddes Smith 1885.

"Two girls W.F.S. had in his eye for the Ball - BLESS 'EM !!"

Inside Briggies. By William Fiddes Smith. 1888.

Main Street:L-R Fergie Keith (shipmaster), John Duffus, Alex Gillespie (butcher), Willie Duncan (Church Beadle and gravedigger).   Photograph courtesy of Betty Wood.

Ivy Jane Moir and Helen Irene Moir at Knockhall ca. 1900.   Photo Jim & Elizabeth Strachan.

Builders at Captain Keith's House in Newburgh.   Photograph courtesy of Betty Wood.

James Brown and Pansy row across for duck eggs 1930.   Photo R. Argo.

The 1996 Grizzlys. Back row: Alison MacDonald, Thomas Ashton, Youth Worker.
Front row: David Moir, Chris Smith, Ryan Gibson.   Photo Sandy & Norma Anderson.

The Hit Squad film the Community Garden. 16-07-97.   Photo Sandy & Norma Anderson.

In 1995, five members of Newburgh Youth Club entered the BP Grizzly Challenge. It was a competition for 14 - 18 year olds, sponsored by BP, which challenged young people to improve their environment in nine weeks.

Over the summer, the team cleared an overgrown wood where they put bird tables and bird boxes and planted flowers to encourage butterflies. They also constructed a walkway around and through the wood and called it the Coull Walkway in memory of Flo Coull who had helped to plant the original wood. The Gruffs, a younger team, upgraded the pavilion and made it accessible for people in wheelchairs.

In November 1995, the Grizzlys won the prize for "Best Presentation" and were presented with a trophy by H.R.H. Princess Margaret. The whole project was funded by local companies with all the work being carried out by team members and an army of volunteers.

In 1996, three of the original Grizzly team with three new members extended the Coull Walkway to join the wood to an observation point on top of the sand dunes overlooking Forvie Reserve. Nearly two miles long, the walkway included a boardwalk to encourage people to keep to the path and not trample wildflowers and marram grass. They also planted over 1000 trees. To raise money to pay for the project, the team produced two booklets, one on the history of Newburgh and another on its birdlife.

The Grizzlys won the BP Challenge in 1996 - an all expenses paid trip to the States.

In 1997, with the help of an army of volunteers, the team made a wildflower garden and a play area on the site of the old tennis courts. The Hit Squad visited the site on two occasions to film progress and the team's efforts were rewarded when they won the Beechgrove Garden's Community Corner Competition.

Roddy Marshall and Jim McCurdy unloading trees. 14-07-97.
Photograph courtesy of Sandy & Norma Anderson.

Sandy Anderson who masterminded much of the planting. 16-07-97.
Photograph courtesy of Norma Anderson.

The Beechgrove Garden Bus.   Photograph courtesy of Carolyn Smith.

Elwin Bremner and the Newburgh Brownies planting the heathers.
Photograph courtesy of Sandy Anderson.

The Public Hall circa 1910.   Photograph courtesy of Dick Fleming.

Fancy Dress Dance in the Public Hall to raise money for the lifeboat 1930s.
Photograph courtesy of Bob Stewart & Carolyn Smith.

The Public Hall was built in 1882 and ever since has been the venue for concerts, plays, dances, meetings, sales of work, Guides, Brownies, Cubs, coffee mornings, badminton, clubs and other village activities.

On the 6th of January 1908, the People's Journal reported:
"SUPPER AND DANCE, An 'at home' inaugurated and carried out by a committee of ladies, was held in the Public Hall on Friday evening. The hall decorations were exquisite, as were also those of the tables. Supper was served at 8.30, and presided over by Rev. J. S. Loutit. Dancing commenced at 10 o'clock, and continued until an early hour in the morning. Gramophone selections were given at intervals. The music was in the capable hands of Mr James Wood. Mr Rose proposed a vote of thanks to the committee and the meeting was brought to a close by the singing of Auld Lang Syne."

Mrs Helen Murray, Pearl Elrick's mother, remembered that in the 1920s there was a gallery at one end of the Hall which was decorated with greenery and little tables were brought in for special occasions. "A proper cosy corner". A great many dances were held at that time such as The Farmer's Dinner Dance, The Golf and Tennis Club Dance, The Football Club Dance, The Ghillies' Ball, The Lifeboat Dance and the Hogmanay Dance. The cinematograph was popular too as was Basket Whist when ladies brought a basket with enough food for two people. The baskets were auctioned and the gentleman who bought a basket had supper with the lady who brought it. At that time the Hall was still lit by paraffin lamp and all cooking was done on paraffin stoves.

In the 1940s Webster's Scottish Players played to large audiences and in March 1949 The People's Journal reported that Newburgh Musical

The Ythan Cronies Christmas party in Briggies 1982. R-L Geordie Wood, Peggy Wood, Rosie White, Dora Mathew, Mona Burnett.

Back L-R Betty Wood, Marjory Donald, Front L-R Madge Kinghorn, Mona Burnett 1985.
Photograph courtesy of Newburgh S.W.R.I

Association had held a social evening in the Public Hall to mark the finish of the winter session. Songs, duets, and choruses were rendered.

One of the many groups which meet in the Public Hall is the Ythan Cronies Club. It was founded in 1982 for the over 60s and is still going strong in 2005. The members meet every Wednesday from September to June to have a chat, play cards, whist or dominoes, listen to a speaker, watch a film, enjoy a fly cup or go on an outing.

Over the years, Moira McIntyre and her helpers have organised the varied programme which has included everything from chair aerobics, a demonstration of Line Dancing, a chance to try water divining and visits to the Maritime Museum in Macduff and the Boggie Woggie Shop in Keith. Every year the Cronies run very

successful fund raising Coffee Afternoons and have a Christmas Party in Briggies.

Newburgh S.W.R.I., founded in 1955, meet in the Public Hall on the first Tuesday of the month. In June 2005 they will celebrate their 50th Birthday with a garden party in Pitmeddan Gardens. The programme is vary varied and includes competitions, talks, demonstrations, visits to and from other Rurals, outings, sales of work and fund raising for charities such Macmillan Nurses, all proving there is much more to the W.R.I. than just jam and knitting.

Newburgh members have demonstrated their acting and singing talents in the many excellent concerts staged over the years. The proceeds of these concerts go to causes such as The Anchor Unit at A.R.I.

Christmas party in the Public Hall 1946.   Photograph courtesy of Richard Argo.

Maisie Wood and George Gray and wedding guests outside the Hall. Early 1930s.

Photograph courtesy of Richard Argo.

Jean Wood & Robert Forester and guests outside the Hall September 1946.   Photo R. Argo.

The Newburgh S.W.R.I. Concert Party. L-R Madge Kinghorn, Betty Wood, Isobel Shewan, Rose Moroney, Mrs Urquhart, Bunty Youngson, Isobel Smith, Violet McConnachie.

Photograph courtesy of Newburgh S.W.R.I.

The Fisherfolk houses on Timmerlum Street and Main Street ca. 1920.   Photo Dick Fleming.

Inch Road in the 1920s.   Photograph courtesy of Dick Fleming.

Newburgh circa 1910.   Photograph courtesy of Dick Fleming.

Knockhall Road 1930s.   Photograph courtesy of Bob Stewart.

Knockhall Castle.

The Udny Vault.

In 1565, Henry, 3rd Lord of St. Clair of Newburgh, an enthusiastic supporter of the Reformation, built Knockhall Castle. In 1633, John, 7th Lord St. Clair sold both the castle and the barony to the Udny family who still own it. In 1639, a party of Covenanters led by Earl Erroll and the Earl Marischal, attacked and captured Knockhall and in the following year it was attacked again by a raiding party from Aberdeen when the laird was not in residence.

The castle was enlarged and altered during the 17th century. There was an L-shaped stair tower, now gutted, on the north side and the kitchen in the basement was vaulted. A circular doocot with a conical roof stood nearby.

At one time there was a courtyard on the south side and the name and arms were on the gate. Over the years rubble from the ruin has been used to build the numerous dry stane dykes in the immediate vicinity.

The castle was accidentally burned in 1734 and has remained a ruin ever since.

The vault, dating from the early 18th century, stands on the site of the old Chapel of Holy Rood dedicated to St. Thomas á Becket. Inside are monuments to the Udny family.

At one time, before the churchyard was enclosed, high tides flooded the burial ground and exposed the bones of those buried there.

Many of the gravestones belong to shipmasters, river pilots and seamen, bearing witness to Newburgh's seafaring past. Unfortunately, the gravestone of Captain John Innes whose ship 'The Oscar' was wrecked off Aberdeen in 1813 with the loss of 42 men has disappeared in recent years.

The name "The Newburgh", still used by some of the older residents of Newburgh, probably dates from the time when the barony of Knockhall or Newburgh belonged to the St. Clair family in the 14th century.

JAMIE FLEEMAN

Jamie Fleeman, known always as The Laird of Udny's Fool, was born in 1713 in the parish of Longside. When he wasn't wandering the countryside, he was the personal servant cum handyman to the Laird of Udny. His eccentric manner and unconventional appearance however, often made him the butt of jokes. Jamie seldom wore shoes or a hat and instead of a coat, dressed in a blue sackcloth doublet. His words came out slowly in a loud nasal voice making him seem simple or roguish, no one was quite sure which.

Hypocrites and bullies were fair game and many an upstart soldier or patronising member of the gentry, who treated him as a fool, soon felt his fist or sarcastic wit. He was immensely loyal to his patron, an inveterate liar, a man of many unreasonable prejudices and a lover of drink and tobacco.

But it was due to his unusual strength that he became a legend in his own lifetime. In 1734, when Knockhall Castle went on fire, Jamie broke into the charter room, picked up the iron chest full of documents and threw it out of the window. Normally it took three men to lift the casket. That same night he also rescued the much-hated housekeeper who gave him only scraps to eat and treated him badly, but in the end he relented and ran up the smoke-filled stairs shouting "Lucky! Lucky! Rise ye auld rudas, or ye'll get twa het hurdies". (two hot buttocks)

There are many stories illustrating Jamie's ability to have his revenge on people who had wronged him in some way. One of the better known anecdotes tells of a gentleman who hailed Jamie to ask where best to ford the river. Jamie, remembering this same gentleman had slighted him in the past, directed him to the deepest part of the river. Some time later, when an irate figure from the far bank accused Jamie of trying to drown him, Jamie replied, "I've seen the geese and the dyeucks hunners o' times crossin' there; and I'm sure your horse has langer legs than the dyeucks or the geese either".

Again, one day Jamie was leading a donkey when a lad shouted, "Is that yer brither, Jamie?"
"Na, na, jist a casual acquaintance – like yersel!", Jamie replied.

Sometime in 1778, Jamie was out wandering the countryside when he was caught in a heavy shower of rain. He took shelter in a barn to dry out, placing a plank against the door to keep it shut. In the morning, the servant lads pushed the door open and the plank fell onto Jamie's head. He was severely wounded and died some days later. His last words were, "I am a Christian. Dinna bury me like a beast."

Knockhall Castle.

Holyrood Chapel 1886 by William Fiddes Smith.

Holyrood Chapel ca. 1900.
Photograph Dick Fleming.

Holyrood Chapel was originally the village school. It was the Rev. John S. Loutit who was responsible for its transformation into a chapel in 1882.

 The picture on the left is probably the earliest in existence showing how Holyrood looked in the early days as it was later re-modelled in ecclesiastical style by church architects, Robertson of Inverness. There were steps on both sides leading up to the pulpit with the harmonium in front. The "rolling screen" cut off an anteroom to the right of the pulpit, which was used for small meetings. The heating was by an ordinary coal grate at the end opposite the pulpit and those who sat at the back were warmest. Dove Paterson provided an acetylene lighting plant,

The tower and clock were added not long after the building became a chapel. A Mr Stewart, a native of Newburgh, who had made his money in Calcutta, offered to present a clock to the village on condition that a suitable place was found for it. With the Rev. J. Loutit in charge, the tower we see today was built and the clock placed at the top.

When it emerged in 1882 that £200 was still outstanding after the tower was finished, the ladies of Foveran decided to hold a bazaar in July of that year. There were seven huge stalls all laden with goods for sale. Mr Udny of Udny opened the proceedings and by 7pm that evening, the debt had been cleared.

In the Foveran Church Newsletter October 1949, Rev R. Robertson announced that the chapel was now lit by the Hydro-Electric supply. In 1948, Miss Keith and her Junior Choir raised £50 towards the cost.

Around 1940 Newburgh was the victim of a minor bombing raid and out of concern for future raids, Major Smith from Newburgh House, who was then Clerk of the Kirk Session, arranged to have the leaded glass panels removed from the windows in the chapel. They were stored in his coach house. This was not recorded in the church records. In 1986, Rev. John Cook was told about the glass and went to Newburgh House to see if it was still there, It was, but beyond repair. What did remain however was used as a model for the replacement glass in the east and west windows.

Charlie Catto with a happer demonstrating how corn used to be sown.

Photo by Sandy Anderson.

There was a mill at Mill of Newburgh in the early 16th century because the conditions of the lease laid out by Henry lord Sinclair, baron of Newburgh to Henry Martyne in 1512 are contained among the papers in the Udny Charter Chest.

It is not the clearest of contracts but the main points are that Henry lord Sinclair was to be responsible for the framework supporting the mill and the channel bringing water to the mill-wheel. He would also compel all his tenants to use only Mill of Newburgh for their corn. Henry Martyne was responsible for all other moving parts and equipment.

In more recent times, Charlie Catto farmed Mill of Newburgh. "Catto's Dairy" supplied milk to Newburgh and the surrounding area and until the late 1940s it was delivered by horse and cart.

In the 1980s the steadings were converted into a dwelling house, now the home of the Gallacher family.

Mill of Newburgh Farmhouse 1923. Flora Catto (grandmother), Flora Catto (daughter), Jane Ann Catto, Isabella Catto. Photograph courtesy of Charles Catto.

Charlie Catto, Rab Yeats and Tom Fraser. Rab Yeats was responsible for firing the furnace to dry the grain. Photograph courtesy of Charles Catto.

David Brown, brother of Margaret Sangster, outside one of the thatched cottages on Beach Road.
Photograph Hazel Stuart.

March Stone.

Tucked away in the grass on the right hand side of Beach Road is a weathered March Stone or boundary marker with 'U' on one side and 'F' on the other.

This stone marks the boundary between Udny Estate and the lands which used to be known as Foveran Estate. It is also very close to the site of the old Poorshouse.

There is a similar stone a little further up on the right hand side near the car park.

"A very WARM DAY."
POORHOUSE:— NEWBURGH.

William Fiddes Smith 1885.

There were four thatched cottages on Beach Road until the late 1930s, home at various times to Pigger Jim Hutcheon, Davie Brown, the Durhams and the Davidsons.

There was also the Poorshouse, where those who had fallen on hard times were maintained by the parish. Patchy Park, Mrs Yule, Lang Lizzie Geddes and Mrs Henderson were among the residents over the years.

At one time, on the other side of the road, on the south west slope of the Gallow Hill, there was a sand quarry known as the Meerie Hill. The tennis courts and part of the golf club car park are now in the open space left behind.

The dunes.   Photograph courtesy of Bob Davis.

Arctic tern.   Photograph Bob Davis.

Female eider.   Photograph Bob Davis.

Forvie was declared a National Nature Reserve in January 1959 after the old Nature Conservancy took a lease from Walker Scottish Estates Ltd who owned the sands of Forvie at the time. The original reserve however only included the sand dunes on the north side of the river.

In the early days, Mike Mathews followed by Malcolm Smith were the warden naturalists looking after the reserve. There were also volunteers such as the tireless Fred Coull and Willie Gall, the same Willie Gall who pulled men out of the river when the lifeboat capsized in 1942.

By the early 70s, Forvie was becoming busier with parties of school children being introduced to the wonders of the reserve - its flora, fauna, landscape, archaeology, bird life and history. It was around then that the old Nature Conservancy became the Nature Conservancy Council.

In July 1973, Aberdeenshire Countryside Committee and Nature Conservancy reported that negotiations were well underway to extend the reserve to take in 900 acres of the Ythan estuary and so protect it from development.

In October 1973 however, it was announced that the quay and warehouses had been sold to a London-based oil service company. The mystery deepened when nobody seemed able to find out the name of the company.

Another potential blow to the future of Forvie came in November 1974 when outline planning permission was sought to build an 80 bedroom hotel and conference centre on the site of the quay. The objectors had an ally in the then laird, Keith Schellenberg, who used a land charter of 1872 giving him the right to veto any project he considered against the interests of the village. Even so, the objectors had a fight on their hands. Sandy

Bob Davis.   Photograph courtesy of Bob Davis.

Eider duck.   Photograph courtesy of Bob Davis

Anderson, research officer at Culterty at the time, summed up their case. "The disturbance caused by large numbers of people walking, motor boating, even shooting would cause terrible damage to the delicate ecology of the area. Years of hard work by scientists at Culterty and the wardens at Forvie to understand and work with the complicated interrelationship between all the forms of plant and animal life on the reserve would be for nothing."

The plans for the hotel were never passed.

In 1979, the estuary was included in the reserve with the unwieldy title of The Sands of Forvie and Ythan Estuary National Nature Reserve. In the 1980s, the name was changed to a simpler "Forvie".

Bob Davis became warden in 1978 and, together with Fred Coull, continued the work of conserving and protecting Forvie as a reserve for wildlife and for people.

Their efforts to introduce visitors to the delights of Forvie quite often had its lighter side. There were lots of "regulars" - schools that came back year after year with different classes. And there was Quarry Hill Primary. As Bob Davis remembers, "A great bunch of kids but always up to something." On one particular visit, Fred Coull had taken them from Waterside, over Rockend and up to Hacklay Bay. Unknown to Fred, two of the boys had come across a herring gull's nest with eggs, and, determined to have the eggs, stuffed them into their rucksack.

On the bus back from Collieston, there was a little "cheep" from one of the eggs and a chick emerged. It must have been on the point of hatching and the heat in the bus and the rucksack did the rest. Fred Coull was

The Ythan Estuary and Forvie.   Photograph courtesy of Bob Davis.

distraught. In the end, the chicks were taken back over the cliffs and returned to their parents, and Quarry Hill went home.

Just as well, Bob Davis reflects, that the boys didn't know about the mines still on Forvie otherwise they might have tried to dig them up.

The whole area was mined during the war and even today there are around 19 beach mines, each large enough to destroy a tank, buried somewhere between the railway carriage and the salmon bothy. At the end of the war when the Army came to clear the mines, the sands had moved so much they couldn't be found.

And Forvie can still yield the unexpected - in the form of coal. Some people suspected a seam of coal just offshore because from time to time quite large quantities would appear lodged among the rocks. Not so. It comes from the old steam driven fishing boats which would leave Aberdeen laden to the top mast with coal because the more they could

carry, the longer they could stay out. The sea would become choppy and some of the coal fall overboard and be taken by the current to Rockend.

In the early days, there were some fairly acrimonious spats between N.C.C. and local people - such as in 1979 when there was a proposal to close the gate at Waterside to prevent vehicle access down the track along the estuary. This was intended to prevent anglers driving down the track, onto the foreshore and continuing on into the eider breeding colonies, not to prevent walkers.

The introduction of bye-laws, such as keeping out of the ternery and only using certain paths during the summer so as not to disturb young birds, caused uproar. At a public meeting in Newburgh, one past resident threatened to shoot anyone trying to prevent him doing what he liked on Forvie.

During the 1980s, Bob Davis and a host of volunteers rebuilt the derelict Little Collieston Croft and made it into the Forvie Centre. They laid boardwalks to encourage people to stay on the paths and made a hide down by the ternery.

In 1998, the Forvie Centre became the Forvie Stevenson Centre as we know it today named after Margaret Stevenson M.R.C.V.S. who left a bequest of £90,000 to Scottish Natural Heritage to fund the new building.

Small pearl-bordered Fritillary on Forvie.
Photograph courtesy of Bob Davis.

*A large part of Forvie is in the parish of Logie Buchan but as the reserve is such an important part of life on the eastern side of Foveran parish, it has been included in this book.

NEWBURGH GAMES
Aberdeen Daily Journal, Monday 6th July, 1908.

"The old-established gathering for athletic games at Newburgh took place on Saturday in beautiful weather and a large turnout of spectators gathered round the ropes of the enclosure on the Links in which various contests were lost and won. The games were held under the patronage of Mr J. H. Udny of Udny; Mr W. J. Chambers-Hunter of Tillery; Major-General Mackenzie of Foveran; and Mr F. Godfrey Hill, Little Haddo. In addition to these there contributed to the prize fund - Messrs Catto, wine merchants. A gold medal was presented by Messrs Williams and Sons, Regent Quay; Messrs Wallace and Company, George Street; Mr John Ritchie, Udny Arms Hotel, Newburgh; and Mr Robert Durham, Ythan Hotel, Newburgh.

The games started at one o'clock and were carried on without a hitch until the programme was completed, under the superintendence of Mr F. Godfrey Hill, who acted as starter; and Mr James Moir, Udny; and Mr George Park, Meikle Haddo, the joint secretaries. The judges were Messrs Alexander Watson, Waulkmill; James Lamb, Westfield; and Donald Dinnie, the champion athlete

who wore a number of his medals and a silver belt. The old man was quite a feature of interest inside the ring, he being still wonderfully active.

The great event of the day was the tug-of-war, open to the parishes of Foveran, Belhelvie, Ellon, Logie-Buchan, Slains and Udny. No fewer than five teams of stalwarts entered for the contest, and the final decision was that Udny came out top. Little Haddo second and Slains third. Newburgh and the Quay were out of it, but it has to be taken into account that the ballot, as well as strength and training had something to do with the result. The teams, in the matter of strength, might have been more equally pitted against each other, but it had been arranged beforehand to abide by the draw. As it was, the top scorers had clear wins.

Apart from the games proper were various kinds of amusements provided by Mr Duckworth, and dancing was also largely engaged in to the music provided by the Grandholm brass band. Altogether the gathering was most enjoyable and successful. Amongst those who visited the ground in the course of the day was Mr Udny of Udny, whilst others came from long distances to be present. Credit is due to the secretaries, the judges and their assistants for the the smooth working of the arrangements, and Mr F. Godfrey Hill deserves a special word of credit for the enthusiasm he threw into the proceedings."

Over the years, competitions included vaulting, the high leap, hammer throwing, wrestling, a married farm servants' race and a single farm servants' race, obstacle races, dancing, the mile race and a hurdle race. Mrs Mabel Aiken recalled that there was also a prize for the neatest hair and ankles. There were sheepdog trials as well but they were less of a success from a spectator's point of view as the competitors disappeared over the sand dunes.

Joseph and Jessie Duncan. Newburgh 1963.   Photo courtesy of National Museums of Scotland.

John Innes.   Photographs Pearl Elrick.

James Innes. B.E.M.

Dr. Joseph Duncan, founder of the Scottish Farm Servants Union its secretary from 1912 until 1945, lived at Witch Hill on Main Street in Newburgh.

He was educated at Robert Gordon's in Aberdeen before moving to London where he worked as a postal clerk. During his time in London, he became interested in the Labour Movement. On returning to Aberdeenshire, he set about trying to improve the lot of farm workers, a cause which made him highly unpopular with many farmers.

In 1945, Glasgow University conferred on him the Honorary Degree of Doctor of Law in recognition of his services to farming. He died at the age of 85 in 1964 and is still remembered as a charismatic and innovative reformer.

John Innes, coxswain of the lifeboat from 1908 - 1931, was awarded the Silver Medal for Gallantry by the R.N.L.I. for his part in the rescue of the crew of the "Imperial Prince" in October 1923.

The R.N.L.I. report from Nov. 15th which dealt with Special Awards reads: "To Coxswain John Innes, who went out on three of the four attempts, although he was injured, the Silver Medal….."

John Innes was in charge of the salmon fishing at the corf house and was also one of the river pilots.

Bowman James Innes was awarded the Bronze Medal by the R.N.L.I. for his part in the rescue of crew of the "Imperial Prince".

During the war he was in charge of the Newburgh Coastguards and in 1952 was awarded the British Empire Medal for his services.

James Innes was the "mussel man" at the Inches and ghillie for the guests at the Udny Arms who came to fish.

James Crombie, pictured left, was a river pilot on the Ythan in the early part of the 20th century, one in a long line of skilled seamen who guided ships into the port of Newburgh. He was also responsible for keeping the flag flying on top of the Gallow Hill.

As a young lad, like so many others from Newburgh, James Crombie went to sea, working mainly on the London Aberdeen trade with occasional trips to Archangel and South America. He married and returned to the village to help his father with the fishing. This he combined with piloting when a vacancy came up in the pilot boat, which at that time required five hands,

On the death of pilot master Robert Brown, James Crombie took over, a post which he held until three years before his death at the age of 81 in April 1931. He is buried in Holyrood Cemetery.

(Left) James Cromie, river pilot.   Photographs courtesy of Dick Fleming.

James Crombie (centre).

James Crombie in a boat on the Foveran Burn.

LOCAL ENTERPRISE.

During the 19th century, the University Medical School paid good money for bodies for dissection. The story goes that one very cold night two gentlemen from Newburgh, one known locally as Resurrection Jack, dug up a recent grave and, placing the corpse sitting upright on the cart, set off for Aberdeen.

At the Blairton Inn (The Cock and Bull), they decided to call in for some refreshment. The landlord came out to get their order.

"Two jugs of yer best," said Jack.

"An' fit aboot yer freen?" inquired the landlord.

"Na, na. He's weel past needin' a drink," came the reply.

THE VERDICT.

Lizzie Geddes, the wayward daughter of Lang Lizzie from Links Street, had a youngster by a German seaman. The baby only lived for a few days and Lizzie said it was a good job it deid as we'd never hiv kent a word it said.

100 PIPERS.

When a local farmer (known to be partial to the odd dram of the whisky "100 Pipers") died, a lone piper led the funeral procession up the road to Foveran Churchyard. His friend watched the cortège and shook his head. "An there he goes, awa' to his Maker 99 pipers short."

William Fiddes Smith 1885.

"ONE FOR THE ROAD".

One evening a group of local farmers returning from the Highland Show in Edinburgh came into Briggies for a "wee cloch an' dichter" ("one for the road"). They'd clearly had a very good day as one farmer was heard to observe, "A've had siventeen cloch an' ditchers since Stonehaven, an' that's a fact."

COURT REPORT 13th MARCH 1900.

Farm Servants' Cantrips. - James Marnoch, farm servant, Waterside Slains and John Smith, farm servant Foveran, were at Aberdeen Sheriff Court yesterday charged with having on the 3rd inst. from the shop of James Keith, grocer, Newburgh, stolen a box containing 56lbs of soap, or, alternatively, with having been guilty of malicious mischief, by breaking the box and scattering the contents on the roadway. Both pleaded guilty to malicious mischief, and their plea was accepted. Mr Thomas MacLennan, procurator fiscal, explained that the shop was one at which farm servants were wont to congregate. On this particular night some of those in the shop pushed the box out at the doorway, and the accused marched off with it. When, however, they found that the box contained soap, and not herrings as they had expected, they broke it, and threw away the soap. They were each fined 25/-, with the option of four days' imprisonment.

(Aberdeen Journal)

THE MINISTER

In the summer the minister's place was taken by visiting clergymen. One of these - a mighty angler - came for the trout fishing year after year and officiated in the pulpit. He was a big man, bald and clean shaven. A long, lipless mouth bisected his massive jaw. He had an impressive manner of thrusting his upper bulk far forward over his hands, clenching the rail of the pulpit and thundering with vehemence the details of Hell. Of him it was told that at the close of one of his lurid descriptions of Hell he intimated to his congregation, "and when ye are suffering all this, ye will raise your eyes to the Lord and ye will say unto Him, "Oh, Lord we did not think it would be as bad as this." And the Lord will look down upon ye and in His infinite compassion and mercy will say unto ye, "Well, ye ken noo."

(The Early Life of James McBey. An Autobiography.)

GUESS THE WEIGHT.

During the 1940s, Cultercullen W.R.I. held an Open Night with a sale of work and a bulb show. The competition at one of these evenings was to guess the weight of a trussed fowl. It turned out that the winner was the person who had donated the bird.

The following day Mr Bews, the headmaster, happened to be looking out of his classroom window when he saw Mrs X going to the shop. He kept watch and intercepted her on the way back to tell her how unfair he thought it was to weigh the hen before the sale.

She heard him out, looked him in the eye and said, "Na Na dominie, that's faur yer wrang. It wisna a hen ava. It wis an auld dane cock."

(Violet Garrick)

CROSSED WIRES.

Mrs Ritchie from Grantleigh once asked a young joiner who was doing some work for her to go to Shanghai (a large house on Main Street). He explained that his firm only went as far as Ellon.

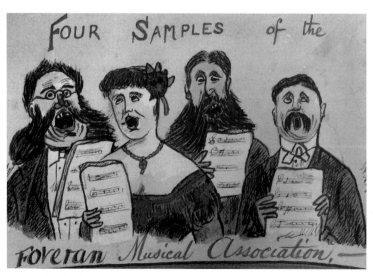

William Fiddes Smith 1886.

William Fiddes Smith. 1886.

FOVERAN

There is the parish of Foveran which stretches from Tillery on the west side to Waterside bridge on the east and there is the area known as Foveran centred on Foveran School and Foveran Public Hall.

Foveran should really be called a village as it has, or has had, all the necessary ingredients. There was the shop at the end of Blairythan Terrace run by Ethel Taylor, there is the school, the hall and businesses such as Eddie Black Plant Hire and Michael Duncan, Builder.

Unlike so many other settlements within commuting distance of Aberdeen, Foveran hasn't changed so very much over the years. Since the 1950s, some of the smaller farms have been taken over by larger ones - Ardgill and Westfield now belong to Savock, Dubbystyle belongs to Cultercullen Farm and Hill of Minnes to Gillanders of Arnage. The parks have been made larger to accommodate combine harvesters and the few derelict cottages converted into modern homes.

Some of the farmhouses belonging to the smaller farms have been sold on together with a few acres to people with an interest in horses or gardening, South Minnes, Kirkhill and Dubbystyle being examples. The council houses on Blairythan Terrace were built in the 1950s where before there were only a few private houses and two farm workers cottages. Only slowly has more housing appeared.

There is still a strong sense of community due in part to the school and also to the Community Club in the hall. The Club started up in the 1950s for the benefit of people of all ages and has been going ever since. Up until fairly recently there were four groups meeting from Monday to Thursday every week - badminton, bowling, drama and whist. Only renovations to the Hall in 2003/4 caused a temporary halt to the Club's activities.

Westfield circa 1900.   Photograph courtesy of Ian & Betty Stott.

Kirkhill 1920.   Photo courtesy of Buchan Heritage.

The opening ceremony of Foveran Public Hall 30th October 1953.   Photograph courtesy of William Mackie.

A Hall Committee was formed in the 1940s with Dad as its first chairman and William Mackie, now at Tullynessle, as secretary. The committee was hard working and arranged many fund-raising functions, mostly held in the school.

A popular event was a Friday Night Concert and Dance. After school the pupils helped to push back the big science table in the Head Teacher's room (at that time Dad taught P7 and S1, 2 and 3) and the desks, opened the partition between the two west classrooms and set up the staging, complete with curtains, at the north end of the school.

Many of the concerts were provided by local talent, sometimes by the school pupils. Dad ran a Youth Club in the school and encouraged the members to sing, with my Mum Agnes as pianist, and to put on humorous sketches.

We children perched on the classroom window sills or the science table where we had a good view of the concerts. I remember, for example, the lovely singing of Rosie (Munro) Barrack and her brother Freddie and the cornkisters sung by George Paterson.

Foveran Public Hall was built in 1953, by coincidence the year of Queen Elizabeth's coronation. Several people, including my father, William Mitchell, were keen to have a public hall in Foveran. Dad, who was Head Teacher for thirty two years, envisaged a hall and playing field near the school where the children could have P.E. and sports and the community could hold functions.

My sisters and I were then too young to go to dances so Mum took us home (next door) after the concerts and while she thought we were in bed, we would sit on the wide window sill of the back bedroom and watch the band and the dancers in the school.

"Main's Wooin' "1952. Photograph courtesy of Christine Fordyce.

"Main's Wooin'." Left: Mrs Campbell from New Deer and Eveline Emslie. Photograph courtesy of Eveline Emslie.

The W.R.I. also raised funds for the Hall through concerts, whist drives etc. They met in the school and Newburgh ladies joined the Foveran ones until eventually a W.R.I. was formed in Newburgh. Later they met in the Hall but unfortunately had to disband about fifteen years ago due to lack of numbers.

Dad also ran a Drama Group for many years. They put on a wide variety of plays, sometimes three one-act plays and sometimes a three-act play, some in Doric and some in English. To raise even more money for the Hall, they toured other schools and halls, often performing on tiny stages.

When my sisters, Enid and Lorna and I were old enough, we were roped in to help with stage make-up or props or to take small parts in plays and I was co-opted to the Hall Committee and Mum persuaded me to take over as pianist for the concerts.

Some of the stars of the plays which took place in the Hall were John Duncan of Mill of Foveran and his brother Leslie, John Stott, father of Ian, Willie and Maud Mackie of Ardgill, Marjory Burnett, (mother of Connie), Ethel Taylor who ran the Foveran Shop with her mother Eveline Emslie, Bill Mitchell of Mill of Ardo and Charlie and Doreen Fowler.

The original site for the Hall was the field behind the school but a snag was hit and it was finally built on Overhill ground thanks to the generosity of the late Eric Buchan. He, his son Eric and grandson Derek all served on the Hall Committee, the late Eric Buchan following my father as chairman. Gladys Rennie did a spell as our first lady chairperson a few years ago.

The Hall was built by William Bruce of Ellon, father of the present Bill.

FOVERAN AMATEUR DRAMATIC COMPANY

— PRESENTS —

"MAINS'S WOOIN"
(A Comedy of Rural Aberdeenshire) by GAVIN GREIG

★

In FOVERAN HALL

ON

WEDNESDAY & FRIDAY
9th and 11th February, 1955

★

ACT 1. *Scene* 1. The Braes—Sunset. *Scene* 2. The Souter's Shop.
Scene 3. Knowhead—Evening. *Scene* 4. The Highway—Night.
Scene 5. Room in Police Station—Late at Night.
Scene 6. Schoolroom—Afternoon.
ACT 2. *Scene* 1. Room in Laird's Mansion.
Scene 2. Knowhead—Evening.
Scene 3. Harvest Field—Mid-day.
Scene 4. Mains of Bungry—Harvest Home Night.

★

CHARACTERS OF THE PLAY.	PLAYERS.
Mr SANGSTER, Mains of Bungry (Well-to-do Farmer)	JOHN STOTT
PETER (Main's Man)	ADAM SHERRIFFS
JOHN MURISON (Shepherd)	WILLIAM F. MITCHELL
Mr BIRSE (Souter)	WILLIAM BARRACK
JOHN ANDERSON (Small Farmer, of Knowhead)	LESLIE DUNCAN
Sir JAMES ROSE (Laird)	JOHN SINCLAIR
Mr THOMSON (Dominie)	Rev. J. TENNANT
POLICEMAN	WILLIAM MACKIE
GAMEKEEPER	JOHN DUNCAN
POACHERS	PETER TENNANT and GEORGE REID
SERGEANT (Army)	STEWART BUCHAN
CHARLES (Page-boy)	DOUGLAS REID
GEORDIE (Harvester)	JOHN SHERRIFFS
PIPER	JOHN W. S. BEWS
Mrs ANDERSON (of Knowhead)	Mrs W. MACKIE
MAGGIE ANDERSON } daughters	EVELINE EMSLIE
JEANNIE ANDERSON }	ISOBEL WYNESS
JESSIE (Housekeeper)	Mrs H. BURNETT
OLD WOMAN	Mrs G. REID
ANNIE and MARY (Harvesters)	MARGARET BEGG and CHRISTINE MITCHELL
HARVEST QUEEN	Mrs J. MILNE

★

CHOIR OF MAIDENS: GIGLIOLA GILLAN, MARGARET FRASER, HELEN BUCHAN, LORNA MITCHELL, EUNICE INGRAM, EILEEN WILLOX, HELEN DAVIDSON, MAUREEN RILEY.

SCHOOLBOYS: COLIN HENDERSON, ERIC BUCHAN, SANDY HUTCHEON, CHARLES SHERRIFFS.

★

Musical Director—Mrs TENNANT.
Prompter—WILLIAM MACKIE, Jnr.
Stage Managers—GEORGE REID, JAMES MACDONALD, ANGUS CUMMING and ANGUS CUMMING, Jnr.
Producer—WILLIAM MITCHELL.
Secretary—WM. F. MITCHELL, Mill of Ardo, Newburgh.
'Phone Balmedie 277.

There was an afternoon opening on October 1953 to which officials and the public were invited. A Concert and Dance were held in the evening and the Hall was crammed.

Dad, and his namesake Bill Mitchell, transferred the Youth Club to the Hall and made it a Community Club for all ages consisting of four groups meeting from Mondays to Thursdays - badminton, bowling, drama and whist.

Dad, Bill and Willie Mackie went into Aberdeen to buy bowls and carpets and carpet bowling was introduced to Foveran. Bill eventually became chairman of the Club and did the job conscientiously for thirty years. Dad continued putting on plays in the Hall.

The Committee had sensibly advised the architect that they wanted a big stage with a slight slope. Many visitors have admired our stage. The Drama Group members made most of their own scenery and props - one member, Charlie Fowler, the Menie blacksmith, also made guards for the hall heaters, large metal ashtrays and car park gates. Foveran blacksmith, Willie Low, acted in plays, played his fiddle at concerts and generally lent a hand.

Two memorable shows were "Main's Wooin" with a large cast and "Jamie Fleeman" in which Graham Hay, as Jamie, and Mabel Duncan gave such moving performances that many of us were in tears. Other productions included "Aunt Janet" and "Kye Among the Corn" which played to packed audiences.

Doreen Fowler recalls the Drama Group going to Ardallie to perform "Aunt Janet". Unfortunately someone had forgotten to bring the wreath,

Foveran Hall Community Club. 1973. Back L - R: Billy Robertson, Dorothy Hutcheon, Christine Fordyce, William Mackie, Anne Riddel, Anne's friend, Michael Norrie, Front L-R: June Duncan and Kathleen Junor.   Photograph courtesy of Bill and Sheila Robertson.

a vital prop in the play. The cast was to be seen hunting the verges for wild flowers minutes before the play was due to start.

In the early days, there was a shortage of men for one particular production and Bill Mitchell from Mill of Ardo was persuaded to help out. He was given the script and learned his lines while out ploughing in his tractor. Much to his surprise, Bill discovered that he enjoyed acting and became one of the Group's most loyal members.

We held many Talent Contests where we "discovered" expert tin whistler Alex Green who was a pupil at Foveran School, and Peter Nicol, a magician now famous both in Britain and abroad.

Another way money was raised before and after the Hall was built was by holding Marquee and Barn Dances. In the early years several farmers kindly lent fields for erecting marquees. We held the Foveran Gala on the first weekend in June for many years. The committee worked hard putting up the marquee, laying our own dance floor, setting out chairs and the school staging and buying food and drink for snacks and teas. Some members, including Dad, even spent two nights in the marquee to prevent theft and vandalism - yes, it happened in the Fifties too!

As well as a Concert and Marquee Dance on the Friday night of the Gala, we tried various things on the Saturday - football and other sports, fancy dress parades, pipe bands, Highland dancing, sheep dog trials and clay pigeon shooting (at which John Duncan from Mill of Foveran was an expert). The Saturday ended with another Marquee Dance. The Hall Committee believed in booking the best bands possible to draw the crowds - we had Jim MacLeod's Band several times.

When the cost of hiring marquees became too high, we held Barn Dances mainly in the steadings at Rashierieve, the inside always scrubbed and whitewashed, courtesy of the Buchan family.

These dances were good fun and raised a lot of money but after several years Health and Safety Regulations came in which meant installing a kitchen in the barn for catering and permanent toilets. We could not afford to do this and had to have all the functions in the Hall from then on.

A new generation of artistes emerged, for example, the daughters of John and Leslie Duncan including the late Aileen who had a beautiful singing

COMMUNITY CLUB BOWLING CHAMPIONS.

Back Row L - R: George Marshall, Doug Riddel, Jim Warrender, Geordie Duncan, Bill Robertson, Billy Duncan and Michael Robertson.
Front Row L - R: Michael Duncan, Alan McBain, Ann Riddel, Catherine Willox, Jean Riddel, Billy Robertson and Bill Mitchell.

Photograph courtesy of Bill & Sheila Robertson and June Marshall.

voice and acted in plays, the Junor girls, the Riddel girls and Michael Norrie, an accomplished young comedy star.

Until 2002 when renovations began, Foveran Hall has been used two to three nights a week. We may not have as many functions as we used to but the Community Club and Hall Committee are still in being, in contrast to some halls built at the same time which have not been used for years and have even been demolished.

We have now installed new toilets, including one for the disabled, new double-glazed windows have been fitted, the floor has been sanded and new curtains hung. We have had new heating installed and the interior has been painted.

Foveran Public Hall is ready for another fifty years of community activities.

Ethel Taylor(centre) kept the shop in Foveran.   Photograph courtesy of Ian and Betty Stott.

Foveran W.R.I. in the 1950s. L-R Back: Mrs Reid, Mrs Pirie, Mrs Mackie, Miss Sangster, Mrs Milne, Mrs Cartney, Mrs Low, L-R Front: Miss Taylor, Mrs Barrack, Miss Emslie. Photograph taken in Foveran School.   Photograph courtesy of William Mackie.

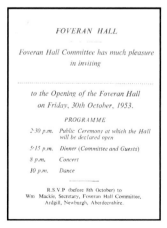

FOVERAN HALL

Foveran Hall Committee has much pleasure in inviting

....

to the Opening of the Foveran Hall on Friday, 30th October, 1953.

PROGRAMME

2·30 p.m.   Public Ceremony at which the Hall will be declared open

5·15 p.m.   Dinner (Committee and Guests)

8 p.m.   Concert

10 p.m.   Dance

R.S.V.P. (before 8th October) to Wm Mackie, Secretary, Foveran Hall Committee, Ardgill, Newburgh, Aberdeenshire.

E. EMSLIE.

FOVERAN HALL FRIDAY 30th OCTOBER 1953.

Iced Melon
Chicken Broth
Cream of Tomato

Steak & Kidney Pie
or
Cold Roast Beef & Salad
Brussel Sprouts:Green Peas
Roast and Boiled Potatoes

Neapolitaine Ice & Fruit Salad

Coffee

W. Geddes – Caterer – York Street, Aberdeen.

Menu for the Foveran Hall Opening.
Courtesy of Eveline Emslie.

Foveran Public Hall 2005.

Foveran Parish Church in 1901 before the apse to accommodate the organ was put in on the south wall.   Photographs courtesy of Christine Fordyce.

There has been a church at Foveran for many hundreds of years. Very little is known about the early church however and it is only from around the mid-1500s that records were kept. We know for example that Thomas Tulliedaff was minister at Foveran from 1582-1632 and that at the age of 98 he asked the General Assembly for security of his pension of 400 merks * a year.

At the Revolution in 1689, the Church of Scotland changed from Episcopalianism to Presbyterianism, although in Foveran Episcopal ways prevailed for a while. The Reverend James Gordon, an Episcopalian, was installed in 1692, being presented by George, Earl Marischal and other heritors. A large number of the parishioners disapproved of this appointment and various attempts were made to remove him. On one occasion, a group of parishioners and a detachment of dragoons broke down the door of the church in an attempt to install their own Presbyterian minister. The Reverend James Gordon was eventually driven out of the parish in April 1696.

* merk: a silver coin worth about 6p

Rev. John Loutit (1880-1912). Rev. Thomas McWilliams. (1912-1931). Rev. Arthur Gordon (1932-1940). Rev. J. Stewart. (1940-1947). Rev. R. Robertson (1947-1951).

Ye Foveran KIRK "Scaling" 1 O'clock

The talk generally at a Country Church is much of a commercial nature; the people come early to have a chat & compare prices & it has been named the Sunday Market.

The Foveran Church music is very antiquated – bad singers & out of tune –

Walking home from Foveran Church after the Sunday Service.
Watercolour by William Fiddes Smith 1886.

During John Gilchrist's long tenure in Foveran from 1727-1815 he sought solace in alcohol. It seems he preferred the alehouse to the church, even on Sundays, and over the years got himself into severe financial difficulties. He was admonished by the Presbytery of Ellon and instructed not to go to alehouses "without urgent necessity".

When William Duff (1755-1815) was minister, the following notice appeared in the Aberdeen Journal in December 1792. Prospective builders only seem to have been given two weeks to tender for the work.

NEW CHURCH TO BE BUILT.

As it is proposed that a new church, fit to contain 700 people, shall be built at FOVERAN as early as the season will permit, to be finished (at farthest) against the first of August, any well-qualified reputable tradesman who is willing to undertake the same, and will find security, if required, for the suitable performance of the work, may give in a plan and estimate of such church, and of the terms on which he will engage, to finish it, to Mr Duff, minister at Foveran, betwixt this and the 15th of January next.

Rev. J. Tennant (1952-1957).

Rev. D. Barron (1958-61).

Rev. T.J. Dyer (1962-1972).

Rev. Robert Wallace (1972-1986).

Rev. J. Cook (1986-2000).

Rev. Neil Gow (2000 -).

Foveran Church in the 1930s when paraffin lamps still lit the church.

Photograph C. Fordyce.

The Churchyard where there are around 270 gravestones.

Photograph Christine Fordyce.

The walls are to be good rubble work. What stones may be needed (excepting rebbits and lintels which it is presumed can be brought at less expense from Murray by sea, than can otherwise be afforded) will be got within a mile and a half of the church. The lime, wood and slates must be brought by the undertaker by sea to Newburgh and will be led from thence by the tenants, who likewise lead the sand. The undertaker is desired to mention the quantity of lime he proposes to use, and the size and quality of the wood. It is also expected, that he should state separately, the mason work and plaster work, both of the walls and roof.

Two years later Foveran Church was finished. It was paid for by the major landowners whose duty it was to provide a church for the people in the parish and pay the minister's stipend from the tithes collected from the tenants.

An excellent picture of Sundays in Foveran parish in the late 19th century is found in James McBey's autobiography when the Reverend J. S. Loutit was minister.

Religiously every Sunday forenoon all the villagers who could walk the intervening mile attended church service - a grim and solemn ritual. A strong smell of confined varnish pervaded the church and lent the service a characteristic flavour.

(The collection) was done by the elders of the Kirk, each of whom went to his appointed section bearing a pole like a broom handle with a square open wooden box at the end, like a cigar box minus the lid. Deftly he pushed this along in front of each pew, the meanwhile everyone listened to the fall of the coin into the box. All could tell if the coin was a half-penny, a penny, or a threepenny piece.

Our minister - the Reverend J. S. Loutit - was determined to change the mode of collection and at his own expense supplied purple velvet bags which could be

Inside the church 2004.

The Flower Festival 1994.

Photograph courtesy of Christine Fordyce.

passed from hand to hand, quietly in a civilised manner. This created a schism and feelings ran high for months. Nearly half the congregation suspected this to be a ruse of the Devil who had caught the minister off guard.

Sundays were dreary days - days of restraint, inertia and suppression. Every physical action was either permissible or sinful and the Sabbath had a code all to itself. No games allowed: whistling, because of its association with joy or light-heartedness, was forbidden.

It was the Reverend Loutit who organised the purchase of the former Newburgh Mathers School which was converted into Holyrood Chapel. On the baptism of his son, John Harvey, in 1885, he presented Foveran Kirk Session with a baptismal font inscribed with the words "Suffer little children to come unto Me". The Reverend Loutit's death in a motor accident at Tipperty in 1812 must have been one of the first such accidents in the area.

On the 5th of June 1994, Foveran Church celebrated its Bicentenary with a re-opening and re-dedication ceremony and the celebrations continued throughout that year with a whole raft of activities. The church was re-decorated and re-pointed, the Women's Fellowship made a commemorative sampler, there was a treasure hunt, a dance in the Foveran Public Hall and an exhibition of artefacts and photographs. Guest ministers such as the Rev. Mathew Rodger, Moderator of Gordon Presbytery, and The Rev. R. Wallace conducted services.

The Rev. John Cook wrote a booklet on the history of the church and special notelets, pencils and mugs were produced. Twenty trees were planted in the glebe and a lectern, carved by elder David Swan, was presented to the congregation. The children helped to bury a Time Capsule in the grounds of the church.

The end of the celebrations was marked with a Flower Festival.

There is a tombstone inside Foveran Church on the west wall commemorating two knights who were probably killed at the Battle of Harlaw near Inverurie in July 1411. The stone used to lie outside the south west corner of the church and would have been inside the Turin aisle in the medieval church. By comparing certain features on similar stones, the slab can be dated from between 1350-1450.

The stone is grey sandstone, approximately 222cm x 103 x 14cm and has a crack across the middle. Unfortunately there are no names or a date and, as the slab seems to have been re-cut at some time, this makes identification of the figures difficult. The only inscription is *hic iace(t)* - here lies.

The fact that the stone depicts two members of the same family suggests they might have died in battle and the only likely conflict in the early 15th century was the Battle of Harlaw. It is possible they were brothers, sons of Andrew Turin, Andrew being the son of William de Turin who was granted the Charter of Foveran by David 11 in 1359.

The hour glass attached to the pulpit is thought to be the one mentioned in an inventory of 1774.

The bust which stands half way up the stairs in the church could be of Sir John Turing, Bart of Foveran. He is in the dress of the time of Charles 1. It stood beside the well in the grounds of Foveran House for many years, then in the hall and was gifted to the church by the MacKenzie family in 1979.

In 2000, the Rev. Neil Gow succeeded John Cook as minister of both Foveran Church and Holyrood Chapel.

For three weeks each month, Sunday service is in Holyrood, on the fourth Sunday it is held in Foveran Church.

The column of the font may have come from the pre-Reformation church at Foveran or even from the Chapel at Hill of Fiddes, no sign of which now remains. For many years it stood in the churchyard before being worked into the base for the font.

"The Foveran Burn" James McBey. (1912).

Courtesy of Aberdeen Art Gallery.

James McBey.   Courtesy of Aberdeen Art Gallery.

James McBey, the Nee-bo-ro loon, who became one of the finest British etchers and landscape painters, was born just outside the village in a cottage beside the old smiddy at Newmill. When he was 4 years old, his grandather died and he, his mother, grandmother and aunt moved into what is now McBey Building in Newburgh.

It puzzled the young McBey that his mother's name was Gillespie when his was McBey. One Sunday afternoon he was taken by his mother for a walk on the Links where they met a tall, thick-set man. On the way home, she told him the man was his father.

At Newburgh Mathers, McBey struggled with arithmetic and Latin but was very good at geography. His visual memory was excellent and, with no effort at all, he could study a map and reproduce it accurately. It surprised him greatly that his schoolmates did not have this same facility. So, when Willie Murray, the grocer, offered a prize of 2/6d for a drawing of Knockhall Castle, McBey studied the ruin until he knew every stone. He won the competition and his work so impressed Nellie MacKenzie, known locally for her oil paintings of flowers, she invited him to watch her paint. He spent an unforgettable day as she mixed different colours and worked at her easel.

Much to the amazement of his schoolmaster, McBey won a bursary of £5 a year for three years. When the first instalment was paid, he cycled the 13 miles into Aberdeen where he bought his first set of oils at James Stephen & Sons, Woolmanhill.

At 14 James had to leave school to earn a living. The Manager of the North of Scotland Bank in Ellon, a friend of both his grandmother and mother, arranged for James to sit the Bank entrance examination. While

McBey at his press. He often wore a long shift when working.
Photograph courtesy of Aberdeen Art Gallery.

he was waiting in the manager's private room before being interviewed, James became so engrossed in a painting on the wall - the first genuine oil painting he had ever seen - he did not hear his name being called. James passed the interview but the bank official was concerned about his apparent deafness.

At the age of 15, McBey became an apprentice at the George Street branch of the North of Scotland Bank Ltd. in Aberdeen, a job which he loathed. In his free time however, he borrowed books on art from the library and by copying the illustrations, began to appreciate perspective and the effect of light and shade. He also enrolled in evening classes at Gray's School of Art.

It was from a library book that McBey learned the technique of etching. His first successful attempts, now the famous boats at "Point Law" where the ferries from Shetland tied up, and "Boys Fishing" were produced using his grandmother's mangle as a printing press. Although delighted with the prints obtained with the mangle, he did not consider them of any value and was flattered to give them away to anyone who wanted one.

An uncle, blacksmith George Gillespie, who had moved from Newmill in Foveran into Aberdeen, helped McBey make a more portable press. The rollers were cut from the discarded steel piston rod of a marine engine found in a junk yard and during the winter of 1902/3, they constructed the new printing press. (George later became blacksmith on the Balmoral Estate at Clochenturn, Crathie and made the wrought iron gates in the Balmoral Garden which bear the initials G.R. & M.R.).

In 1910, after eleven years, McBey left the Bank with no regrets. He wanted to make a living as an artist but, although the good citizens of Aberdeen liked his etchings, no one was prepared to buy them.

That same day he left Scotland for Holland where for the next two months he toured art galleries and museums, painted, sketched, talked with other artists and absorbed the culture of the country.

McBey wanted his work shown in London so when the art dealers Goupil & Co. said they would take his work on sale or return at a commission for themselves of over 66%, he went to London in May 1911.

Goupil's agreed to put on an exhibition in November 1911 for which McBey made 20 new plates. "Few attended", he wrote in his diary on the first day, the 21st of November. Two days later Goupil's had sold 29 prints and 77 by the 6th of December. The exhibition was a resounding success and McBey never looked back.

McBey in the desert.   Photograph courtesy of Aberdeen Art Gallery.

"Strange Signals".   Courtesy of Aberdeen Art Gallery.

He was commissioned as a Second Lieutenant in 1916 and sent to Army Printing and Stationery Services in Boulogne. During his time in France, he produced a series of dramatic etchings epitomising the futility and tragedy of war.

In March 1917, Campbell Dodgson, Keeper of Prints & Drawings at the British Museum recommended him for appointment as Official War Artist with the British Expeditionary Force in Egypt. Once there he worked tirelessly drawing prisoner-of-war camps, the Port-Said docks, Ismailia and the desert, travelling around as best he could in canal boats, on foot or in open railway trucks.

He went with the advance troops through Syria and Palestine and on a 5-day reconnaissance with the Australian Camel Patrol into the Sinai Desert, made the drawings on which "Dawn - The Camel Patrol Setting Off" was based.

In the years after the war he travelled to Spain, France, Italy and Holland before sailing to America in 1930. It was there he met the beautiful Marguerite Loeb. They were married quietly in New York in March 1931 and sailed for England that same day.

They were again in America at the outbreak of the Second World War. The authorities impounded Marguerite's passport and they had no choice but to remain in the States for the duration of the war.

For the last ten years of his life McBey lived and painted in Morocco. But he never forgot his Newburgh and North-East roots and returned on several occasions, the last time in the spring of 1959, shortly before he died.

"The Blacksmith's Shop" James McBey (1902).

Courtesy of Aberdeen Art Gallery.

James McBey (1952).   Courtesy of Aberdeen Art Gallery.

The smiddy at Newmill, Foveran. George Gillespie is holding the work on the anvil and his assistant is 'Chapper' James Hastie.

Photograph taken by Rev. J.S. Loutit.

On the wall of his bedroom in Spain hung a section of the large-scale Ordnance Survey map showing the parish of Foveran.

After his death, McBey's friend and patron, Harold H. Kynett presented 204 prints to Aberdeen Art Gallery. When Kynett himself died in 1973, it was found he had left 79 etchings and watercolours to Aberdeen University. He may have assumed that the same authority governed the Art Gallery and the University. Happily, the University agreed this new collection should go on permanent loan to the Art Gallery and as a result, Aberdeen now has the finest collection of McBey's work anywhere in the world.

McBey's Building in Newburgh where James McBey spent his childhood.

Willie Low was blacksmith at Newmill Smiddy in Foveran from 1934 until he retired at the age of 74 in 1977. In his younger days, Willie's job was mainly shoeing horses but as farms became more mechanised, it changed to welding and engineering. As one of the first users of the electric welder in the parish, he straightened the propeller shaft of a steamer at the quay in Newburgh, made grass rollers for Aberdeen University's playing fields and a coal separator for Mitchell & Rae.

Sandy Anderson remembers that inside the smiddy the floor was completely covered in pieces of metal and there were boxes of bolts at the far end where Willie's pet chicken had built a nest.

James McBey lived in the house at Newmill Smiddy and Willie met him on several occasions when he returned to visit his birthplace.

Willie took an active part in the life of the parish. He was a founder member of the Foveran Hall Committee and a member of the drama group. He was also an elder of Foveran Church for 32 years and president of the Ellon branch of the Master Farriers and Blacksmiths Association. Willie carried out much of the maintenance work on Foveran House for Miss MacKenzie.

On his retirement, Willie sold his business to Davie Wilkie.

Golden Wedding celebration. P&J.

Willie Low.　　Photograph courtesy of P&J.

The house at Newmill Smiddy 1998.
Photograph courtesy of C. Fordyce.

Newmill house at the time of James McBey.
Photograph courtesy of Aberdeen Art Gallery

Foveran School 1955.   Photograph courtesy of Christine Fordyce.

Foveran School 2005.

In 1873 the Rev. Mr Clark and the Rev. Mr McKay, members of the School Board, introduced the new headmaster, Mr Hugh Lee, to the pupils of Foveran School. Mr Thomas Smith was his assistant teacher.

The headmasters of all three schools in the parish were required to keep accurate attendance registers. These registers had to be inspected at least every three months by a member of the School Board. Attendance percentages were submitted to the Board every month and the figures for each of the three schools in the parish were carefully scrutinised by the respective headmasters.

A constant cause of concern for Mr Lee was the number of absentees and he was careful to record the reasons in the logbook. All pupils walked to school in those days and heavy falls of snow soon blocked the roads making them impassable. Illnesses such as scarlet fever, scarletina, flu and whooping cough were common and frequently caused class numbers to fall. And twice a year at term time, when farm workers and their families moved on to another farm, the roll went down until new families came on to the register. There was the hairst and potato lifting time too when the older children were needed to work in the fields.

But there weren't always legitimate reasons for absenteeism. On the 30th of July 1875, Mr Lee noted in exasperation, "The attendance is still very irregular owing to the carelessness and indifference of parents."

Between the 1870s and 1890s the curriculum included History, Reading, Spelling, Dictation, Domestic Economy, Physical Geography, Recitation, Arithmetic, Needlework, French, Latin, German, Greek, Religious Knowledge, Geometry, Literature and Composition.

Foveran School before the safety railings and the new extension.

Photograph courtesy of the P&J.

A Government Inspector came annually to monitor progress and for weeks before his visit, the pupils received "special drilling" in various subjects. In 1876, the Inspector's Report read:

"The lower classes in this school made a good appearance in Standard subjects. Written work of higher standards was also well done, but under oral examination, the fourth standard though generally up to the requirements in grammar, want readiness in Parsing and Analysis, while the fifth standard were decidedly defective both in Analysis and Parsing. An attempt has been made to instruct too many of the scholars in English Literature and Physical Geography and the result has been that majority presented failed to show by any means intelligent comprehension of the subjects. Mathematics, French and Latin have been taught with more success to fewer pupils. The time spent on English Literature and Physical Geography would have been more profitably employed in developing the Scholars' general intelligence which was barely passable throughout."

In August 1878, Mr Lee was appointed Rector of Campbeltown Grammar School and Mr John Anderson became headmaster.

By 1890 the Inspectors were able to give the school a glowing report. "This School has made a highly distinguished appearance. Order and General Tone excellent."

Mr William Williams M.A., who had been Classical Master at Kilmarnock Academy, was appointed head teacher in October 1892. The school roll was 78.

At the beginning of 1893, the school was closed for five weeks due to an outbreak of measles. When it reopened on February 7th however, there were still a great many pupils absent and the Compulsory Officer was called in to find out the reason. It seems there was "Still a good deal of sickness."

In September 1897, the Rev. Loutit introduced Mr James Watson M.A. as head teacher. He spent the first week trying to find out how much the pupils knew but with half them still absent and unlikely to return before the harvest was finished, he had to be patient for a few weeks.

The problem of overcrowding was addressed in 1899 when a new Infant Room was added over the summer holidays. It took until the end of the year to complete however and until then all classes were held in the Large Room. Mr Watson noted, "….on account of the noise made by the joiners, little progress has been made."

Miss Easton and pupils 1919 .   Photograph courtesy of John and Ina Duncan.

Attendance figures in December were poor. "The weather has been stormy and some of the children suffer from colds; but there are many who are absent from school without sufficient reason."

In November 1899, drawing was being taught on slates and "the children take a very great interest in it."

In 1904 when the school roll was 84, new distractions tempted some pupils to miss their studies. Early in 1903 Mr Watson wrote that the attendance was average and "much reduced on account of a ploughing match on Tuesday and steam mills and other attractions during the week."

There was always rivalry every year between the three schools in the parish when it came to the results of the Mathers Bursary Competition. Mr Watson was delighted in 1906 when Foveran pupils took the first three places. He was less impressed with Class Junior 11, the highest in the Infant Room, when he tested them in April 1914. "The results were by no means satisfactory. Reading was indistinct, monotonous, and not very accurate, spelling was poor, the average number of mistakes in dictation was 4, intelligence was practically nil, while answering in Geography was poor. Arithmetic was only fair, oral work being very slow."

The School Board put great emphasis on Religious Knowledge and at frequent intervals during the school year, visiting ministers arrived to test the children.

As all pupils walked to school in those days, some coming from as far away as Mill of Minnes and Newburgh, the weather, particularly in the winter, affected attendance. Those who did get there were often soaked through and had to sit round the fire to dry before any lessons could begin. On the colder mornings, they were given brose for breakfast with three pupils eating out of the same wooden bowl. There were no school dinners in those days but the children were given a cup of cocoa to drink.

In an interview for The Ellon Times in 2000, Mrs Mabel Aiken recalled that in the years immediately after World War 1, the children would pull old socks over the top of their ankle boots to prevent the snow getting into them. The problem of cold, wet feet was still a matter for concern in 1945 when Mr William Mitchell was headmaster. "Few children," he wrote, "have Wellingtons and the quality of other types of footwear is so shoddy that few pupils reach school with dry feet. Every effort is made to get their feet dried in school as soon as possible."

Burns Supper in Foveran School 1953. The haggis bearer is Mrs Marjory Burnett. Seated L. to R. are, The Rev. John Tennant (half hidden), Mrs Milne then Mrs Ena Buchan.

Photo courtesy of Christine Fordyce.

On November 14th 1941, the log book reveals that the teachers "were occupied in issuing Pink Ration Books……Interruptions in teaching on other days was slight: although dealing with Clothing Coupons (supplementary) with higher pupils caused some break in the work."

During the war years everyone was encouraged to grow vegetables, and Foveran School was no exception. From 1940 onwards, the boys dug and planted out the school garden. In June 1942, Mr Logan H.M.I.S. came to inspect their efforts and Mr Mitchell noted, "There is now a considerable area of ground under intense cultivation, and there is promise of good results for the season."

The girls knitted socks, scarves and gloves for the Forces and the headmaster observed that, under the guidance of Miss Law, they had produced some very fine work.

The pupils also collected paper and metal for the war effort.

In May 1945, the pupils were given two days holiday to mark the end of the war in Europe and again in August when the war in Japan came to an end. In June of that year, Mr Mitchell wrote, "The effect on the attentiveness of children of Double British Summer Time is noticeably deleterious, the long light evenings obviously robbing many children of their due sleep."

At the prize giving at the end of the summer term in 1945, prizes in the form of Saving Stamps from the funds of the Sarah Anderson Trust were presented by Mr David Harvey, a former pupil who had recently returned from a German P.O.W. camp.

Mabel Aiken said she always had plenty of company going to school. At the end of the farm roads, she and her friends would make a mark to let other children know that they had passed that point. There were no tarred roads in those days so it was easy to scrape a line with the heel of a boot.

The first references in the log book to the Second World War affecting the day-to-day life of the school appear in the entries for 1940. In August the head teacher Mr Mitchell wrote, "Drill in taking cover below stairs, proceeding to corridor and cloakroom, and putting on respirators occupied some time during the week." And again, in October the same year, "Mr McNaught, Assistant Director of Education, called for a few moments on the question of window protection."

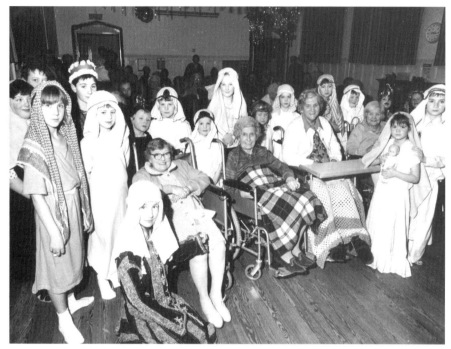

Nativity Play 1987 performed for the patients in Morningfield Hospital.   Photograph P&J.

Before the Public Hall was built, the school was used for drama productions and other social functions such as the Burns Supper shown in the photograph. Early In 1948, the headmaster wrote that a play was being staged so all the furniture in the primary classroom had been rearranged. The school also had a visit from Mr H. Mitchell, the Drama Advisor, who called to discuss adult and youth dramatic activities.

That same year the older girls started domestic science classes at Ellon Academy and the boys began woodwork. There was also an extra holiday to celebrate the Silver Wedding of the King and Queen.

But the headmaster was not happy. In December 1948 he wrote, "The Secondary Division has never been so devoid of pupils that gladden a teacher's heart, but they are well behaved and they work with reasonable diligence."

In 1978/1979 renovation was being carried out at the school so all 31 pupils, head teacher Mr Sutherland and Assistant Teacher Mrs Morrison started the new session in August at Tipperty School. They remained there until the 6th of June 1979.

During Mr Sutherland's tenure, there were a great many educational visits to places such as Towie Barclay Castle, the Art Gallery to study James McBey, Beauty Hill to explore the source of the Foveran Burn, Haddo Country Park where the children rowed in punts on the lake and to local churches to learn about different styles of architecture.

In May 1983, as part of a study on pollution, P6 and P7, complete with rods and worms, made a trip to the Foveran Burn to take samples of the water and do a bit of fishing. Caroline Cumming caught a ¾lb trout.

Mr Sutherland retired in 1990 and was succeeded by Mrs Barrett. In 1991 there were 31 pupils but by September of that year it had risen to 47, entitling the school to three teachers.

In October 1993, Mrs Barrett attended the funeral of Mr William Mitchell, head teacher of Foveran School for many years.

In January 1996 the whole school moved once more to Tipperty while the long awaited extension was being built. In October the same year, a foul smell was reported coming from the Early Stages Room. Floorboards were lifted in an attempt to find the source. The cause - a pair of trainers!

In April 1998, when Mr Colin McLean was head teacher, the School "internet multimedia computer was installed."

During the last weeks of the 20th century, when it snowed heavily, the children performed the musical nativity, "Rock around the Flock" to senior citizens and went to see "Beauty and the Beast" at His Majesty's.

In March 2000, Mr MacLean presented the Rev. John Cook with a book and a framed photograph of his last official duty in the school to thank him for his hard work over the years. In May Mr MacLean too left Foveran School and Mr Stuart Seivwright took over as head teacher.

In February 2002 the BBC Radio programme "Grass Roots" was aired and some of the children heard themselves giving an opinion on "What makes a good farmer's wife?" In November 2002, the school won £1000 for school funds after coming 3rd in the P&J Disney Trip Competition. The money was spent on two new printers and a trip for the children.

The new extension 1996.   Photograph courtesy of Foveran School.

Caroline Cumming & her friend Morag in May 1983 when Caroline caught a ¾lb trout in the Foveran Burn.

The new extension completed.   Photograph courtesy of Foveran School.

Foveran School 1992.

Photographs courtesy of Foveran School.

Mr Sutherland retires 1990. Mr William Mitchell, Mrs Barrett, Mr Sutherland.

School Sports 2003.

Scottish Dance Festival 1993.

Auchloon circa 1910.

Photographs courtesy of Buchan Heritage.

Frogmore circa 1910.

Linnhead circa 1910.

Savock circa 1910.

Foveran has always been predominately a rural parish. The land is fertile, these days producing barley, some wheat and oats, oil seed rape, neeps and potatoes. Sheep and cattle do well on the grassland and there is a large pig rearing establishment at Pitmillan.

Since the 1900s, mechanisation has brought about huge changes in farming in the parish. In the 1920s and 1930s, horses gave way to tractors for pulling ploughs and binders. There was the mobile threshing machine such as the one owned by John Duncan from Mill of Foveran, there were better milking machines, balers, muck spreaders, drilling machines and these days the highly sophisticated combine harvester can cut, thresh and bale a 100 acre park in a matter of hours.

Such innovations, and many others, have meant that these days only a few people are needed to work the land. The photograph taken at Aikenshill before the First World War shows just how many men were needed for haymaking. It was hard physical work and the orra loon, the lowest person on the farming hierarchy, has brought out refreshment to the men. The hand-pulled rakes held by the two workers on the left were called smilers.

In the photograph taken at Hill of Minnes, the grieve is standing alone. On his right is the orra beast, the horse used for odd jobs or extra power. The men with the pairs of horses are the farm servants responsible for ploughing and for looking after the horses.

Before threshing machines were invented, the men were up at 4a.m. flailing corn (oats). They would feed, groom and muck out their own individual pair of horses before having breakfast themselves. Then, provided the ground was not frozen or sodden, they took their horses out to the fields to plough for as long as there was enough light to see.

Aikenshill circa 1910.

Hill of Minnes circa 1910.   Photographs courtesy of Buchan Heritage.

Savock circa 1910.   Photograph courtesy of Buchan Heritage.

Watercolour by William Fiddes Smith. 1886.

In the earlier part of the 20th century, unmarried farm workers lived in bothies or chaumers. These were often cold, dark places beside or above the stables. The entrance was from a rickety ladder and trap door. Bothy men prepared their own food whereas chaumer men ate in the farm kitchen. The better bothies had an open fire with a swee which was a metal device for swinging a kettle or pot over the flames. They drank tea from billy cans similar to the ones in the photograph.

The basic diet was oatmeal with milk and potatoes supplied by the farmer. The men made the oatmeal into brose which they ate from a wooden bowl called a caup using horn spoons. The bowls are shown in the photograph.

The men are sitting on kists or chests which would have contained all their possessions - best clothes for Sundays and perhaps a musical instrument such as a fiddle. They are wearing clothes typical of farm workers around the First World War - heavy tackety beets, waistcoats, corduroy trousers tied under the knees with nicky tams (buckled leather straps), and, with one exception, flat caps.

Married men lived in tied cottages or cottar houses and were allowed a small piece of land at the back called a kail yard to grow vegetables to supplement the family's diet. Wives were expected to work on the farm especially at harvest time and were often employed to look after the poultry. The condition of many of these cottages concerned Dr Paterson of Inverurie who wrote in 1891 that in bad weather "many cases of bronchial trouble have scarcely a chance of recovery on account of the impossibility of keeping out draughts from defective roofs, doors and windows".

Cottar families were large and an older daughter might go into service either as a kitchie deem or maid while her brother found work on another farm or went to sea.

Employment, in particular for single men, lasted from one hiring fair to another. When a family moved at term time, the new employer would send one or two carts to transport them and their possessions. At "term" the countryside was criss-crossed with carts on the move.

Binders began to appear on farms from the 1850s onwards. The early machines only cut the corn and left it on the ground for the back breaking work of gathering by hand. Later machines had a device which tied the corn into stooks.

The stooks were built into stacks or rucks where the corn was stored for the winter and, as feed for animals was needed, a section was removed and threshed.

In the 1930s tractors replaced horses for pulling binders until both were replaced in the 1960s by the combine harvester. The larger farms stopped using the threshing mills and replaced them with driers and the stack yards in the corn yards began to disappear as did the art of building watertight stacks.

Dutch barns were built to keep the bales dry and now the big round bales are lifted brought inside by one man using the hydraulic system on the tractor.

Top left: Jim Aiken & Ernie Price at East Knockhall with the binder 1956. Photograph courtesy of Chris and Jim Aiken. *Top right:* At Kincraig. 1950s. Back: Sandy Davidson. Centre: Ian Macauley, Rev. John Tennant, George Gall. Front: Ian Stott. Photograph courtesy of Christine Fordyce. *Middle left:* The tractor Mill of Newburgh. Photo C. Catto. *Middle right:* Alfie Stuart of Bridgefoot with his Suffolk sheep. Photo Hazel Stuart. *Bottom:* L-R Sandy Davidson, John Stott, Ian Macauley, Sandy Willox 1953.

One Day Event at Tahuna 2003.

These days making a living farming is more difficult than it was as the government no longer guarantees a minimum price for grain. As a result, several farmers in the area have diversified into other areas while making use of existing land and facilities.

Norman Davidson from Aikenshill and Alistair Sinclair from Fiddesbeg have planted several hundred acres of trees.

Shelley Johnston and family from Foveran Farms have built up a horse livery business and constructed a competition level cross country course where One Day Events and other horse-related activities are held. They also have a shop which sells horse feed and equipment.

In between competitions, the sheep keep the grass down.

Sandy Ingram holding a home cured gammon.

Sandy Ingram sells home cured gammons and bacon both in his shop at East Pitscaff and in the markets in Peterhead, Banchory, Aberdeen, Inverurie and Stonehaven.

The bacon is cured the old fashioned way using salt and sugar with no added brine. It is left for three weeks then cut into slices and vacuum packed. Sandy also sells cooked gammons and a range of sausages.

The shop opened in 2005.

The Store.   Photo courtesy of Pat Booth.

The Booth family from Savock opened The Store in July 2002. The beef sold in the shop comes from Aberdeen Angus cattle fattened on their own land and it is prepared for sale on the premises. The meat is also sold at the growing numbers of Farmers' Markets held in Aberdeenshire and can also be ordered via The Store's web site.

The Store sells locally grown fruit and vegetables, smoked salmon, bread, oatcakes and a large variety of other products from Scotland.

Betty Stott from West Latch, just across the road from The Store makes the chutneys, pickles, jams and marmalades.

The Booths also offer Bed & Breakfast at Savock itself.

The Buchans at the turn of the 20th century.

The Foreman, Eddie Buchan, Eric Buchan, Roland Buchan and the Grieve hyowing neeps in the 1920s.

Eric Buchan Senior age 14.   Photographs courtesy of Eric and Lena Buchan.

Hairst in Foveran Church glebe 1994.   Photograph courtesy of Christine Fordyce.

Mrs Annie Stuart stookin' at Davishill in the late 1950s.

Photograph courtesy of Ann and John Stuart.

Cutting corn at Overhill in the 1950s.   Photo courtesy of Eric and Lena Buchan.

Eric Buchan Snr. Overhill 1946.   Photograph courtesy of Eric and Lena Buchan.

Mill of Fiddes by William Fiddes Smith 1886.

Mill of Fiddes in the 1930s and 1940s was an arable farm and would not have been considered a big place. The land bordered on Fiddesbeg, Kinknockie, Kincraig and, separated by the Foveran Burn, Savock and Hill of Minnes.

The farmer for the latter two, and Mill of Fiddes, was Leslie Wishart. He did live for a time at Hill of Minnes then later went to Balcairn, Oldmeldrum, but visited the farms regularly.

The grieve stayed in the farmhouse. My father, Alexander Cowie, who was shepherd, occupied one cottar house and the horseman, occupied the other. The farmhouse was a two-storey building with access to the upper flat by a wooden outside stair on the wall facing the road. This flat may have been let from time to time and in 1936 or 1937, when our house was in dire need of repair, we were moved in there. It seemed so spacious in comparison to the cottar house.

The repairs consisted of new windows and doors, the box bed was removed and a small kitchen/scullery built on at the back. There was even a sink and a rotary pump for the water supply. Before that, water was carried from a pump across the road and a few yards along the fence.

The perquisites or perks as they were called were considered part of a farm worker's wages. These were milk, coal, tatties and oatmeal. We had extra meal as the dogs had to be fed on that. Bairns and dogs thrived on a natural diet. A pit was made in the yard before the supply of tatties arrived. They were then covered with straw and earth to keep out the frost and a trench was dug around the pit to drain any water.

Two or three milking cows were kept on the farm for the supply of milk which had to be fetched from the farmhouse about 7p.m. On a bad wintry night the horseman would bring both his own and ours when he went to feed and water the horses about 8p.m.

The coal was delivered by a firm at Newburgh, the coal having come directly there from the north-east of England.

Holidays for farm-workers were unheard of until the late 1930s but at most farms there was a rota so that a Sunday off was available now and again. New Year's Day was the only "official" holiday, and even then animals had to be attended to.

Feeding cattle filled the byres and court during the winter. The grieve attended to this. These kye were fed on neeps, which had to be cut up, and on silage which was grown on the farm and filled into the tall, concrete silo at the corner of the cornyard next to the steading. Silage consisted of peas, beans, tares and clover.

In the late spring or early summer, the byres were empty. We never queried where the cattle had gone. I suppose they went to the slaughterhouse.

The silo was empty and young and old alike heaved their way into the silo - someone usually had an accordion or mouth organ - and we would have a dance. Of course, it was a bit smelly. Farm smells were not considered unhealthy.

An iron stair ran the full length of the inside of the silo. A young single man who had been working on the farm was about to be married and the night before was the customary time for his' feet washing'. He was very brave and climbed to the top and stayed there until the men went away. Actually, it was more a blackening than a washing.

"Dragging Coles" was something we enjoyed. After the hay was turned with the 'Tumlin Tam' then built into coles, came the time to drag the coles to the edge of the field to be built into a haystack or ruck.

A long length of rope attached to the horse's harness was run round the base of the cole. With a child on the horse's back, the cole was then dragged to the ruck. There must have been an art in building the coles as they never disintegrated.

When stooks of corn were dry, they were carted to the cornyard, the area between the steading and the road. Building a cornstack was a highly skilled job and a yard full of them was a lovely sight.

For drying and storing corn sheaves, Mill of Fiddes was one of the few farms where there was a rack. This ran the length from a gate opposite the

John Stuart of Davishill, winner of the Sir John Fleming Cup for the best built grain stacks or rucks in September 1959.   Photograph courtesy of Ann and John Stuart.

farm road entrance almost to the cottar houses and was constructed from a series of upright poles, probably old railway sleepers with wires at different levels running through them. There were two sides about 12 feet apart. The roof was of corrugated iron and there were sleepers at ground level a few yards apart. The sheaves could be fed between the wires even in wet weather. When the rack was full, it was quite dark inside but we thought it an adventure to go "down the rack" and take care not to trip over the ground supports. Of course, it would serve no useful purpose these days but it did play a big part in our childhood.

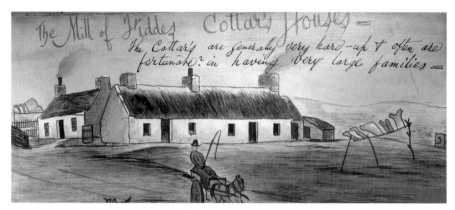

The Mill of Fiddes Cottar's Houses —
The Cottar's are generally very hard-up & often are fortunate? in having very large families —

Cottar Houses by William Fiddes Smith 1885.

After the harvest was over when all was safely gathered in, the barn was cleared up to have a harvest home barn dance. Folk came from some of the neighbouring farms. It was never a big company but with music, singing and dancing, and of course eating, a good time was had by all.

Threshing day was always an occasion. Bill Lamb from Udny Station had the Steam Mill, or "The Stem Mull" as it was known. Farm workers from other farms came to help. The grieve's wife had to do the catering. To this day, I think of a surplus of food as being "enough to feed a stem mull".

The straw was kept for animal bedding, the corn was milled and the chaff was used to fill our mattresses, the old chaff emptied out of the old sack before the milling was finished. What a lovely high bed we had that night. It was probably quite flat before the milling came round again.

As shepherd, my father was more or less his own boss and he was a good conscientious person in looking after the sheep. He did not have much time for horses and less for cows. His life was outdoors for shepherding was a fulltime job.

There were sheep at Mill of Fiddes, Savock and Hill of Minnes that he attended. The night before dipping day, we helped to carry water from the dam to fill the dipper. It was fascinating to watch him with his oilskin coat on back to front putting the sheep through. The policeman, who had cycled from Newburgh where he was stationed, made his compulsory visit at dipping. We didn't go too near while he was there.

The lambing was done at Tillery. The trees there provided a natural shelter belt. Father and his lambing shepherd bothied there for several weeks until the lambing was over. The sheep had to walk there of course. No such luxury as floats or lambing sheds then.

While he was there, after Greig's van from Tipperty had been, mother would pack a basket of supplies and the two of us would walk to Tillery.

We would tidy up the bothy, clean out the ashes, sweep the floor, make the bed etc and after we had our tea with the men - always a boiled egg which tasted better than at home - we would set off for home again. Walking all that way never seemed to be any hardship.

For winter feeding the sheep were usually put into a park of neeps. This park may have been let from another farm miles away. Before the sheep were put there, a cartload of stakes and nets would have gone ahead. This was so that a portion of the field was staked off for that day's feeding and moved again until the whole park was eaten up.

Father would cycle to wherever the sheep were at first daylight and come home in the darkening, very often just having a bottle of tea kept warm in a cloth and a piece to see him through. The advent of the vacuum flask was a boon.

When he realised it was too long for the dogs to run behind his bike on a long journey, he had a box fitted to the front. Eventually he graduated to a motorbike and sidecar, the sidecar being for the dogs of course and not for his wife and family - although they did get a hurl in it now and again.

In fine summer weather, mother and her neighbour would light a fire at the back of the house, place a big stone at either side and set the big washing pot on them. We enjoyed carrying water from the pump across the road. It didn't seem to be the chore it usually was, fetching water for ordinary household use.

Children living on a farm need no designated play areas and we were no exception. There was always space at the rear of the house for the girls to have "hoosies", and with the hens and the ducks to feed, pet rabbits or guinea pigs to look after, we were never bored.

As well as playing around the farm steading, there was also the Foveran Burn where we spent many a summer day paddling. There were two deep pools in the burn but we knew to keep clear of them.

One day at the burn, we came on this duck sitting on eggs. We thought it a good idea to take her and her eggs up to the house and make a nest for her in the shed. She was fed and watered every night, just as the clocking hens were, and, in due course, the eggs hatched out. When the ducklings were a few days old, we decided to give the duck a bit of freedom and let her out into the yard. She did not take long to take advantage of this and, with her brood waddling on behind, headed straight back to the burn - an early lesson in "Don't tamper with Mother Nature".

Interior of a Cottar House by William Fiddes Smith 1885.

The Stem Mull from Udny Station.
Photograph courtesy of Bill Johnston.

Mill of Fiddes Farmhouse 2005.

The steadings at Mill of Fiddes were converted into a dwelling house in the 1990s.

Although we did not have bicycles, the rim of an old wheel made a splendid "gird" and we could clock up several miles running with this. The art was to keep it moving.

Most farm servants had the ambition that one day they would have a place of their own. In 1945, School Croft, between Darrahill and Auchloon became vacant, and the Laird of Tillery offered my father the tenancy. So, after twenty years at Mill of Fiddes in the parish of Foveran, the family moved and took up residence in the parish of Belhelvie.

After we'd been there for some time, my father remarked out of the blue that if he got very drunk one night (which was most unlikely) and had to find his own way home, it was to Mill of Fiddes he would head for. Perhaps that summed up the feelings of us all.

Violet Garrick.

Violet Garrick was born at Mill of Fiddes, the seventh child of Alexander and Beatrice Cowie. In the 1930s, Violet went first to Cultercullen School and then to Foveran Junior Secondary for three years.

After leaving school, she worked at Balmedie Eventide Home before training as a nurse. In 1948 Violet went to Lerwick where she practised as a midwife. Violet married Bobbie in 1950 and now lives in Gott on Shetland.

Since the age of 14, Violet has been a very active member of the W.R.I.

William Fiddes Smith was a keen fiddler and played at dances at Briggies with The Foveran Quadrille Band.

From early life WFS had a great dislike of country life and could not stand more than a day of it at most (or so he thought) but alas! fate he had to do it and the natural result got to like it which shows again one can get accustomed and be contented what're his lot may be.

Foveran is a rather bare sort of county with poor things of trees but grows good crops and the inhabitants are really nice people and WFS is grateful for the opportunity he has had of making their acquaintance.

WFS left Aberdeen in Nov/84, first on a visit to Mr Nicol of Dubbystyle (now deceased), stayed there about four weeks, and had a very pleasant and happy time of it indeed. Afterwards removed to Mill of Fiddes - a two-pair-of-horse-farm with a large old fashioned house and occupied by a widow Mrs Thomson, here WFS was very lonely as he had no companions, but afterwards he got acquainted with some natives and the time passed by more pleasantly.

"A Portrait of the Parish of Foveran" contains photographs of watercolours painted by William Fiddes Smith. The watercolours are contained in two volumes and are a unique record of life in the parish in the 1880s.

Inside the first volume, William Fiddes Smith gives his reasons painting them, at the same time giving an affectionate portrait of the parish. (He refers to himself as WFS.)

"The following pictures were got up by WFS at Mill of Fiddes 1885/86. They were painted for the purpose merely to convey an idea of life in that region, also of the scenery. WFS having a good deal of time on his hands at this time - in fact having nothing to do at all, conceived the grand idea of becoming an artist although he had no previous training……

WFS found the inhabitants to be rather 'stiff' and cautious at first but after-a-bit when they had got at his pedigree and satisfied themselves that he was not dangerous then he had every freedom with them and has been treated in downright proper style.

Since leaving WFS has paid a good many visits to Foveran and finds great pleasure in again making up to his old friends and having a chat with them."

"There being a very large 'loft' at this place and the farmer Mr Stott being of an obliging disposition; Balls and Dances took place very often and it is needless to say were always kept up with great vigour to the sma' hours."

The owner in 1886 was Andrew John Mitchell Gill whose maternal ancestors had been at Savock for 150 years. He was a J.P. and Commissioner of Supply for the counties of Aberdeenshire and Elgin. At one time, Savock or Saak belonged to the family of Turing of Foveran.

The steel cables in the right of the picture conveyed power to a threshing mill at the farm from a water wheel in a hollow at the dam quarter of a mile away. The cables were taken away when they proved too low for double decker buses to pass underneath.

In the 1880s, the Harper family lived at Westfield. They sold the farm to the Stotts of Kincraig. In 2000, George Booth from Savock bought Westfield from Ian Stott and today it is the location of the farm shop known as The Store.

Born at Rathen in 1913, he worked on farms around the Fraserburgh area before moving south to work as cattleman for the late Eric Buchan Snr. at Rashierieve. He lived with his wife and three sons in one of the cottar houses next to the now disused filling station on the main Aberdeen road. Eric Buchan Snr. was heard to observe that there was something different about David Toulmin. He often appeared distracted – perhaps planning his next story.

In those days, Toulmin had no car, relying instead on his bicycle to get around locally. He often made use of the abundance of public transport for trips into Aberdeen to the library or to the cinema travelling in buses belonging to companies such as Alexanders, Sutherlands, Burnetts, Simpsons and Cruickshank & Ross.

In the late 1950s, the family moved round the corner to Aikenshill where Toulmin became orraman then tractorman to the late Norman Davidson Snr.

His first collection of short stories, "Hard Shining Corn" published in 1972, established him as a Scottish writer in the tradition of Lewis Grassic Gibbon, Charles Murray and Jessie Kesson. Other works include "The Tillycorthie Story", "Travels Without a Donkey" and "The Clyack Sheaf" in which he documents the origins of Foveran House.

In recognition of his contribution to the literature of the North East, David Toulmin was awarded the honorary degree of Master of Letters by Aberdeen University in 1986 at the age of 73.

He died in 1998 at the age of 84.

David Toulmin.   Photograph courtesy of Eric Reid.

David Toulmin was the pseudonym for John Reid, author of 10 books, countless short stories, plays, poems and articles who lived and worked in the parish of Foveran from 1950-1970. Such was his feeling for the parish which inspired some of his best writing, he requested his ashes be interred in Foveran Churchyard.

Foveran House.   Photograph courtesy of the P&J.

MISS FLORENCE MARY MACKENZIE

The elegant central block of Foveran House was built in 1771 by John Robertson, a wealthy stocking merchant from Aberdeen, much of the stone coming from the ruined Castle of Foveran which had stood nearby. The rectangular two-window single storey wings, the Turing Tower and the stuccoed addition over the porch were Victorian additions designed by architects Mathews and MacKenzie.

The Robertsons occupied the house until 1857 when Andrew, grandson of John Robertson, sold off most of the estate. The house and 40 acre policies went to Christina MacKenzie, daughter of Major-General Roderick MacKenzie of Glack. She in turn left it to her cousin, Major-General Roderick MacKenzie of Kintail and Seaforth. His daughter, Florence Mary MacKenzie, who died unmarried at the age of 94 in 1973, was the last resident laird of Foveran House.

Many older residents of Newburgh still remember the small, fiercely independent lady who lived with her housekeeper in the large secluded house half a mile or so from Newburgh. A striking figure often dressed in a tartan cape and wide brimmed hat, Miss MacKenzie could sometimes be seen in the village on her way to visit her friend Major Smith at Newburgh House or going to the Udny Arms.

Her early years were spent at Charles Street, Mayfair with her father. Between the wars, Miss MacKenzie went to Germany to study music where she had tea and dined with Hitler at Berchtesgaden. On her return to London, she associated with people such as von Rippen Tropp, Germany's ambassador to England, Neville Henderson, British ambassador to Berlin and Edward Mosely, leader of the British Fascist Party.

During the Second World War, the house in Charles Street was bombed so Miss MacKenzie moved up to Scotland to stay with Brigadier Crawford on the Norton Estate near Dundee. Foveran House had been requisitioned by the Army with officers living in the house and servicemen billeted at Home Farm.

The story goes that on her birth, the Duke of Cambridge gave Florence MacKenzie a considerable annuity. Her father, realising that if she married, this would become the property of her husband, kept her away from any eligible suitors and accompanied her everywhere. How much truth there is in this story is not known. During conversations with her lawyer however, it emerged that the relationship between father and daughter had been a difficult one.

When Miss MacKenzie came to live permanently at Foveran House, her lifestyle changed radically to that of a recluse without many friends. Casual callers were not welcome and any visitors had to make an appointment in advance. They were greeted by Miss MacKenzie wearing white lace gloves before being shown into the ballroom to sit by a large coal fire. Tea or a half pint tumbler of whisky were offered.

Willie Low, blacksmith and handyman, was one of the few local people allowed into the house on a regular basis. He was even provided with his own pair of slippers for when he came to carry out maintenance work or just to sit and talk. She insisted he call her Flossie.

Professor George Dunnet from Culterty Field Station was anxious to have permission to trap small mammals in live traps for teaching purposes in the woodland surrounding Foveran House. Students were shown the animals and then they were released back into the wild. Miss MacKenzie, for reasons only she knew, decided that Professor Dunnet was " a vivisectionist" and forbade him from entering the grounds. She did however permit Sandy Anderson to take the students there.

Two cakes and softies were ordered every day but never eaten. Instead, they were placed on the end of the kitchen table in a long line. When fresh cakes arrived, these were added to the line and the ones on the end fell on to the floor. A cooked salmon given to Miss MacKenzie by Mrs Bates from the Udny Arms Hotel remained on the window sill for several weeks.

1903 On the steps of Foveran House. Miss MacKenzie seated.   Crown copyright: RCAHMS.

1903 Walking on the beach at Newburgh.   Crown copyright: RCAHMS.

After her death from a brain haemorrhage in 1973, it took many years to wind up her estate. A sad consequence of this delay was the time it took for her casket to be buried. There was no room in Foveran Churchyard and it was only when her solicitor bought a plot in the new cemetery some twelve years later she could finally be laid to rest.

Her estate was considerable but then so were the death duties. Much of the furniture was sold at auction by Christie's. The paintings, some of which were valuable while others were found to be excellent fakes, were sold separately.

Two interesting finds by her solicitor were a diamond and pearl fastening reputed to have been part of the crown jewels of Catherine the Great of Russia and a Louis XV1 diamond and sapphire brooch, both authenticated in London. These were sold by Christie's in Geneva for £30,000.

In her will, Miss MacKenzie's specified that the monies from the sale of her possessions should go towards setting up a trust fund to enable Canadian students to study medicine or related sciences in the UK or in the USA. She thought that Canada had been neglected by Britain during the days of the Empire and the trust fund would go some way towards making amends for this oversight.

After Miss MacKenzie's death, the house stood empty and neglected for several years. Vandals stripped the lead from the roof and the grounds became overgrown.

Foveran Estate was bought by Walter McKinlay of Rockhall Estates Ltd in 1976. In 1982 planning permission was granted to turn Foveran House into a conference centre.

The interior was stripped and refurbished while every effort was made to retain the original character of the building. In 1985 permission was granted for the conference centre to become an hotel.

In 1989, Rockhall Estates sold Foveran House to Rockhall Scotia Resources Ltd, a company which also belonged to the McKinlays, and the house was leased out to be run as an hotel.

Hays Holdings Ltd then acquired the property in a takeover and held it for a short time before selling it as it did not fit in with their portfolio. It was acquired by A. J. Sangster in 1995 and sold to Dr and Mrs Dolman in 1999.

Mill of Minnes was a water-powered corn mill driven by an overshot waterwheel 0.91 by 3.66m. This view shows the waterwheel from the south west, with its wooden launder and fittings intact. The end of the launder is curved to direct the stream of water into the buckets of the wheel. The lever above controlled the flow. Photograph J. R. Hume.

Mill of Minnes in the late 1970s.   Photograph J. R. Hume.

Mill of Minnes was the meal mill for the west side of Foveran parish and in days gone by the tenants of Tillery would have been "thirled" or compelled by law to use this mill.

The present mill, which is small by Aberdeenshire standards, was built between 1800 and 1810 and altered and extended around 1900. It was still in use in the 1960s. Five mills in the area - the Mills of Ardo, Minnes, Fiddes, Foveran and Newburgh - were all worked off the Tillery Burn and the Rack Burn which come together at Mill of Minnes.

Andrew Watt came as miller in 1888 but died a few years later. His son Dan, who took over from his father, had very poor eyesight and eventually became totally blind. Known locally as "the blin' fiddler", Dan was greatly in demand to play at local dances with The Foveran Quadrille Band. It was said that Dan always knew who was approaching because he recognised the rattle of the harness. If it was murky or dark when people came to the Mill, he always carried a lantern because, as he said, "You blin' buggers need licht."

During Dan's time, the Mill of Minnes was used for both weddings and wedding receptions.

Dan worked until he was 72 when he sold the Mill to the Green family. He died a year later leaving around £4000, a considerable sum in those days.

Alan Green recalls the time when his brother Alex, the famous tin whistler, lost two fingers at the age of five in mill machinery. There was no safety guard yet Dan Watt, though blind, never injured himself.

The mill had its own electricity generating plant long before Hydro Electricity came to the parish in 1949.

In recent years the Mill has been converted into a dwelling house. The original mill wheel can still be seen.

Alex Green at the harbour at Portknockie.

Alex Green, the famous tin whistle player, was brought up at Mill of Minnes. At the age of five he lost two fingers in the mill machinery so, unlike his brother and sister, wasn't able to have piano lessons. Instead, he took up the tin whistle and now plays and teaches all over the world.

Alex went first to Cultercullen School and then to Foveran School in 1942. It was wartime and he remembers that all the windows in the school had mesh netting over them to prevent shattered glass falling on the pupils should a bomb fall. One day in 1943, Mr Mitchell the headmaster looked out of the window when he heard the drone of German planes coming in over Newburgh. He shouted to the children to take cover just as bullets began to rain down on the school. Alex remembers to this day how frightening it was hearing them "skiting off the roof".

In the 1950s the Foveran Hall Committee organised Talent Competitions and Alex was one of the performers. He remembers playing his tin whistle often accompanied by Christine Mitchell (Fordyce) on the piano. In December 2004, Alex returned to Foveran Hall with his wife Madeline to give a concert in aid of Hall funds.

After training as a mechanic and two years National Service in Germany, Alex became a lecturer in motor vehicle mechanics.

When Grampian T.V started in the 1960s, Alex joined the programme "Bothy Nichts", then the "Inglenook" series. He joined Jack Sinclair's Show Band at His Majesty's Theatre and in the 1980s played in the Music Hall with Fulton McKay. One Hogmanay he was on both the BBC and Grampian at the same time. Alex still performs, holds workshops and records CDs. He now lives in Portknockie.

John Duncan was born at Montammo in 1917 and began farming Mill of Foveran in 1945 when he bought the Mill, a house and cottage, some animals and the land from brother and sisters Gordon, Annie and Jean Marshall for £2,200. Water had to be carried from a well and there was no electricity until John himself put it in.

Mill of Foveran is known locally as "The Garden of Foveran" because the land is so fertile. Three feet below the surface the soil is still black.

The farmhouse dates from around 1607 and is one of the oldest properties in the parish. The Mill, shown on the left, was no longer functioning in 1945 but John was able to restart it and for a few years ground corn there. Unfortunately, the workings were destroyed by a fire. John's wife Ina remembers looking out of the window and seeing the flames shooting out through the open mill door. Sadly, the mill wheel survived the fire only to be stolen a few years later.

John Duncan 1950s.   Photograph courtesy of John and Ina Duncan.

John was one of the first farmers in the parish to own a threshing machine and for 35 years he threshed corn all over Foveran and beyond. The mill had rubber tyres and one day during the war, he was driving the past the school on his way home when a tyre burst. The bang was so loud, the local air-raid warden thought a bomb had dropped.

For as long as he could remember, John Duncan was fascinated by clocks. Sometimes people gave them to him but more often than not he bought them at the Mart and took no notice of Ina when she pleaded, "Dinna bring hame nae mair clocks." With infinite patience, sitting at a table in the kitchen, he restored them and as John could never bring himself to sell any of them, they remain at Mill of Foveran. There are over 80 clocks scattered throughout the house.

The Mill 2005.

The portable threshing mill which John Duncan operated.   Photograph J. R. Hume 1976.

Mill of Foveran Farmhouse.   Photograph courtesy of Christine Fordyce.

Water diving was another of John's many skills and over the years he found springs and water pipes for farmers all over the parish. He took a twig from a tree and when he felt "the stick twist roon inside the bark", he knew he had found water.

For many years John did all the maintenance work for Alex Wishart at Hill of Fiddes, the first farmer to put fat cattle through the mart in Aberdeen. He recalled that at the back of the house at Hill of Fiddes there is a park called Chapel Park, the site of Chapel of Fiddes which has long since disappeared. Some of the stones from the chapel are still in the cornyard however.

In his time, John won many cups both with a horse and a tractor at the ploughing matches held around New Year time. The men would draw lots for a strip as some strips were better than others.

Mr Watson was headmaster at Foveran School when John was a pupil there and he had Perfect Attendance Cards from 1928 and 1930. He won the Newburgh Mathers Bursary Competition and a 1st Class Certificate from the United Free Church in 1929.

During his 87 years, John saw huge changes. He remembered seeing 80 steam lorries queuing to fill up at the watering place at Blairython and cattle being walked back from the Mart in Aberdeen to Foveran.

Sadly, John died in June 2005 shortly before "A Portrait of the Parish of Foveran" was published.

Jopp Chambers Hunter at Cultercullen School. Photograph Mrs Moira Massie.

At one time, the Estate of Tillery was part of the barony of Foveran and belonged to the Turings.

Early records are patchy but from 1510-40, Andrew Udny owned the estate. Then, around 1650, the Setons of Minnes acquired the property and built a house.

Sir Samuel Forbes is recorded as owner early in the 18th century. It seems he had very definite ideas about architecture because not only did he rebuild the house, he also constructed an elaborate system of flowerbeds enclosed by gates which were decorated with a variety of birds, animals and pious inscriptions. Unfortunately none of his creations survive.

In 1750 the estate exchanged hands once again, this time going to James Ligertwood, a magistrate and merchant from Aberdeen.

John Chambers became owner in 1788. In his youth, Chambers emigrated to South Carolina where he made his fortune, and on his return bought Tillery Estate for £9,500. He rebuilt the house in a classical style, complete with pillars, and added Hunter to the family surname.

The last member of the Chambers-Hunter family to live at Tillery was Jopp Chambers-Hunter. After Charterhouse, he served with the Seaforth Highlanders in France where he lost an arm in 1916 and was discharged from active service. A spell as a tea planter in Ceylon and a government post in West Africa followed before he returned to live permanently at Tillery in 1927.

Jopp was a benevolent landlord and all those who knew him or worked for him liked him. Few however were impressed with his political sympathies. Between 1936 and 1939, he was one of the chief exponents of fascism in Scotland and an active member of the B.U.F., Sir Oswald Mosley's British Union of Fascists.

The citizens of Aberdeen didn't make life easy for Jopp when he tried to convert them to his way of thinking. Before he even started to make a speech at the Castlegate in 1937 he was heckled and pelted with stones.

Tillery House circa 1900.   Photograph courtesy of Elaine Moffat.

Although relays of fire trucks came from Cultercullen two miles away, it was too late. The house was completely destroyed. Only the quick thinking of Ryrie, a local carpenter, who climbed up into the roof space and prevented the fire from spreading through into the servant quarters, saved that part. Other people braved the flames to rescue some of the antiques.

The house was not insured so there was no money for re-building. Jopp had little option but to move into the servant accommodation. He had the inside of the main house re-pointed and was able to use the original pillared entrance to gain access to his new quarters.

Over the years he had collected and planted specialist trees from all over the world in the Sheep Park at Tillery. When, in the gales of 1958, most of these trees were blown down, Jopp seemed to lose heart and moved into 57 Beechgrove Terrace in Aberdeen where he died not long afterwards.

For some years a tenant lived in the property and then it lay empty. The house was bought by the Moffat family in 1986. They have restored the servant quarters and made them into a family home. The shell of the original house still stands next door, a reminder of a bygone age.

There were some ugly scenes and several arrests were made.

Jopp continued to work for B.U.F. until March 1939 when he suddenly resigned his position as the Fascist's National Inspector for Scotland after a disagreement over policy with Sir Edward Mosley. He was fortunate to leave the party when did as many other members were put in prison during the war.

In June 1939 tragedy struck when a maid drying clothes in the attic of Tillery House accidentally started a fire. The Fire Brigade was called but, due to the exceptionally low rainfall that year, there was insufficient water to put the fire out quickly.

Tillery 1966.   Photograph courtesy of the P&J.

Sir Edward Mosely (centre) on a visit to Tillery in 1935.   Photo courtesy of Elaine Moffat.

Tillery in the 1930s.   Photograph courtesy of Elaine Moffat.

CULTERCULLEN

The Smiddy is the great Centre for gossip and "Stories" —

The farrier in this picture by William Fiddes Smith is Mr Dick 1886.

1952

Photograph courtesy of the P&J.

At 30 m.p.h., it takes just 19.1 seconds to drive from one end of Cultercullen to the other. "The Howe" as it known to the locals, is the smallest settlement in Foveran. It was a grouping of small crofts, one or two of which still exist today. Thirteen of them were absorbed into either Cultercullen or Thistlyhill farms and local people used to say that when the smoke from the kitchen fires in those farms went up, another thirteen fires were doused.

A combination of memories of pupils at Cultercullen School and the details recorded by the various headmasters in the school log book, give a picture of life in and around The Howe over the years.

The income from a croft was not enough to keep a family so crofting was often combined with a small business. There was the soutar, the joiner opposite the school, the shopkeeper and the smiddy.

The shopkeeper in the early part of the 20th century was Sandy Mair or "Shoppie Sandy" as he was known. He was very thin and lived with his stout housekeeper, Elsie Brown. It was said locally that she always ate from the fat side of the plate. There was always a big kebbock of cheese sitting on the floor of the shop and Sandy would cut off a piece as customers required. He had to go out the shed at the back though if either paraffin or syrup was needed.

In the 1930s the shop was owned by Johnnie and Mrs Florence but it was "Shoppie Lizzie" who served behind the counter. It amused the schoolchildren to go in and ask "Fit's the price o' yer penny apples?"

Circa 1900.   Photograph courtesy of Mrs M. Stott and Charles Esson.

1920s Mrs Dickie (nee Keag) is the teacher.   Photo Charles Esson and Mrs M. Stott.

Moira Massie remembers being sent to "Shoppie Lizzie's" to buy rich tea biscuits for the teachers' break.

There were the joiners George Mathewson and Mr Mitchell who, when they first came to The Howe, made wheels for the farm carts. They would roll them across to the smiddy to have the rims put on. In the 1930s, horses were still being used on the farms and in the classroom the schoolchildren knew the distinctive smell coming from the forge when Mr Bruce was shoeing.

Other small businesses came later. On the site of the smiddy there was JRD, for example, and at the end of the village Kenny Innes built horse boxes and made parts for the oil industry until the late 1990s.

Back in the 1870s, Cultercullen School had 31 pupils and was in a ruinous condition. A new school and schoolhouse were built in 1873 with Mr John Rose as headmaster, an appointment he held until 1911. It seems Mr Rose may have been somewhat irascible on occasions. In 1881, the father of assistant teacher, Miss Wilson, made a complaint (unspecified) and she resigned. Her successor, Miss Taylor, also left after a disagreement, but Miss Duff, the next assistant, was made of sterner stuff and finding Mr Rose's rudeness unacceptable, complained to the School Board. He was asked to be more courteous in future.

Mr Rose served the school well for 37 years. He developed the Science Courses of the South Kensington Syllabus and some of his pupils passed the examination, a great achievement in those days. His dedication was appreciated and in February 1901, at an evening meeting at which nearly 100 people of all grades were present, Mr Rose was presented with a valuable gold watch and chain, while Mrs Rose received a gold ring.

1938: Back Row L-R: Betty Stephen, Christabel Barclay, Annie Napier.
Front Row L-R: Helen Wilson, Elspeth Paterson, Mrs Christie (cook), Annie Philips, Violet Cowie.
Some of the older pupils who helped serve the school dinners and wash up afterwards were given tuppence on a Friday by Mrs Christie, the cook. "We didn't feel rich that day, we felt we had made our fortune," said Violet Cowie.   Photograph courtesy of Violet Garrick (Cowie).

The log book records that many of Culltercullen School pupils came from large cottar families where the father was "feed" on an annual basis. At "term", when the families moved on to another farm, the school could lose up to a third of its pupils at a time. New families came into the area however and the roll would rise again.

The Education Act of 1873 made attendance at school compulsory until the age of 14 and the head teachers of all three schools in the parish were required to submit attendance figures to the School Board every month. Mr Rose noted in November 1901 that the attendance of the older boys was below average, accounted for by The Feeing Mart in Aberdeen and potato lifting time.

At harvest time too absenteeism was often a problem when some pupils were kept at home to look after younger brothers and sisters as their mothers were required to help with the hairst.

On Wednesday April 10th 1910, Mr Rose reported that the joiner's shop opposite the school had caught fire and the older boys helped to put out the flames by carrying water from the school taps and the burn. The school was closed on the Friday to mark the King's funeral.

By the time Mr Rose retired in 1911, there were 127 pupils on the roll. His successor was Mr Jason Gordon Souter who served from 1911 to 1915.

Overcrowding was a problem and a report by H.M.I.S. in 1914 suggested that better use be made of available space. "The large infant room, certified for 118 pupils, might easily be divided into two by a partition. This would necessitate the appointment of an additional teacher, which would make for efficiency and relieve the present over-crowded room."

After Mr Souter resigned, possibly to join the army, Mr J. A. Morrison was appointed in August 1915 at a salary of £192. 3/- plus the schoolhouse. Although he received call up papers, he was granted exemption from military service.

In February 1916, Mr Morrison gave the senior pupils written tests in composition and arithmetic. He found the arithmetic results disappointing and resolved "in the case of certain pupils to punish smartly careless errors."

In October of the same year Mr Morrison wrote: "Miss Falconer has received a note from Mrs Christie, Mill of Fiddes. The note is scribbled on

1937.   Photograph courtesy of Mrs Moira Massie.

1938.   Photograph courtesy of Mrs Moira Massie.

the exercise book of one of her pupils. She demands no more home lessons and threatens withdrawal of her children from school."

The log book entry for November 1916 reads: "Some children have been taken to Maud Poorhouse in order that their bodies may be cleansed of vermin."

It is interesting to note that Christmas Day was a school day, although work did stop early to allow the head teacher to address the pupils. They sang a few carols before being dismissed at the usual time. Moira Massie and Jeanette Meacham remember making Christmas decorations in school in the 1930s and being puzzled that there were none at home. Christmas was not celebrated at that time in Scotland.

In November 1917, Mr Morrison received a letter from Mrs Rae at Auchloon saying that she could not send her children to school during the winter if the right of way was ploughed up by Mr Lamb. Mr Morrison referred the letter to the Clerk.

In February 1921 the Sanitary Authority informed the school that there were three members of one family in the area with diphtheria. A few weeks later, Dr Watt visited the school and recommended the rooms be wiped over with a solution of Lysol. The pupils were warned not to drink directly from water taps.

He returned in June to take swabs from the throats of some of the pupils and a week later the school was closed.

In the days before mass immunisation, the logbook contains frequent references to pupils being absent due to flu, mumps, measles, scarlet

Schools always need more money and Cultercullen was no exception. One imaginative fund-raising effort took place in the late 1970s when Ian Marr (third right) from Cultercullen Farm held a ploughing match with a difference.

Taking part were L-R: James Irvine, Craibadona, Alfred Stuart, Bridgefoot, William Rae, Rosebank, Eric Stanley, Logiemuir and Ian Williams, Logierieve. The money Mr Marr paid the men for their work was donated to Cultercullen School funds.   Photograph P&J.

fever, diphtheria, whooping cough, bronchial troubles and chicken pox. Every now and then the headmaster recorded the death of a pupil.

In 1935 he wrote, "It is with regret it is to be noted that James Taylor, Woodside Terrace, Udny Station, died in the Isolation Hospital, Fraserburgh of Scarlet Fever."

As late as 1938, H.M.I.S. reported that in Cultercullen School "Epidemic

sickness and the usual term changes which affect about a third of the school population annually, have hampered the work, but nevertheless creditable results have been achieved."

An ongoing problem at the school was the water supply or the lack of one.

In 1911, Mr Rose complained that the supply had completely dried up and that water was having to be carried from a neighbouring well - "though the quality of same is not all that could be desired."

There was no improvement by 1917 when Mr Morrison sent a complaint to the Clerk, Mr Lindsay. In 1921, his successor Robert Thompson wrote: "The only water supply for school and schoolhouse is got at an open well some distance from school and as children occasionally throw objectionable matter into it, and even commit a nuisance in it, a proper supply should be seen to as soon as possible."

In May 1923, the head teacher was able to report that a new supply had been introduced but by 1925 the problem reappeared. In September it was noted that there was only "sufficient water to flush the latrines once this week (Thursday), flow stopped since." The supply failed again many times in the following years and well into the 1930s the boys had to carry water to the school from a burn which ran past the playground.

During Mr Thompson's tenure from 1921 to 1924, the school was extended to accommodate the rising number of pupils.

Mr Bews taught at Arnage before coming to Cultercullen where he served from 1924 until 1963.

1979.   Photograph courtesy of Cultercullen School.

coal fires had to be cleaned out in the mornings, the ashes emptied into the ash pit at the back of the boys' toilets, firewood and coal had to be brought in and the fires lit before the school opened.

Mr Bews' methods of instilling discipline were all his own. On one occasion he caught Hilda Fraser and Violet Cowie from the Infant Class having a scrap. He simply marched them round to the cookery room, lifted them both up and deposited them into the big boiler. Fortunately, as Violet points out, it was a cookery lesson going on and not laundry day.

Play sheds were erected around 1935, one for the boys and one for the girls. There was a wooden seat running along the back. Violet Cowie remembers that on the first day of the new sheds she was looking forward to sitting down after the long trek to school. The early arrivals beat her to it however.

In the early 1930s, the pupils put on pantomimes such as Cinderella (Margaret Fullerton from Millton of Minnes was one of the ugly sisters) in the Udny Station Hall.

Until the 1950s, the pupils used slates and a skallie (a slate with a slate pencil) for any written work. Each child had a clootie for wiping their slates and at the end of each summer term, the clootie had to be taken home and boiled.

After school, the children often helped with peat cutting on the moss at Darrahill and Craibadonna. Each tenant of Tillery had his own lair supervised by the Moss Grieve, Andrew Yuill.

Violet Garrick, Moira Massie and Jeanette Meechan all remember the pupils from the Tillery area following a path alongside the burn to get to

He had a fine singing voice and sometimes entertained at local events. Mr Bews was less inclined than his predecessors to record much more in the log book than attendance percentages and numbers on the school roll. On the 22nd of April 1930 however he wrote "Took custody of coal cellar key from Cleaner on account of excessive use of coal for year 1929-30."

Each classroom was heated by a large enclosed American stove. A map of the world hung above it. The children often brought containers of milk to school which were placed round the stove to warm up, a practice which put Jeanette Meechan off milk for life.

The school cleaner's job was not an easy one. There were four classrooms, the cookery room and three cloakrooms to clean. The outside toilets had to be flushed as there was no way of flushing them as they were used. The

159

Cultercullen School before the extension.

school. They came "ben the burnieside" which could be dangerous, especially after heavy rain, but did save many miles. Jeanette Meechan still recalls being terrified by the big black snails which used to appear out of the long, wet grass.

At the end of the year "The Tattie Ball" was held in Udny Station Hall to raise money for hot dinners for the children Everyone came in fancy dress and one year the local joiners, Mr Mathewson and Mr Mitchell, appeared as Laurel and Hardy.

Empire Day on the 24th of May was still observed in the 1930s. On their way to school, the children would chant," The 24th of May is the Queen's birthday. If we don't get a holiday, we'll all run away."

The piano was dragged out into the playground where the Union Jack was flying. The children stood in a circle singing "All Hail the Flag of Britain" before parading past the flag, the girls bowing and the boys saluting.

In May 1936, the school was given a talk on South Africa by Mrs Botha, daughter-in-law of Boer General Botha. Mrs Botha was brought to the school by Jopp Chamber-Hunter from Tillery who presented all the boys with cricket sets.

In March 1939, a wireless was installed in the school, a "Murphy 5 Valve Radio purchased from Neil Ross in Ellon."

In January 1942 there was a heavy snowstorm. Mr Bews wrote "Train stuck at Newmachar. Work terribly handicapped during this storm."

At break time, the boys often played marbles while skipping was popular with the girls. They would sing "On the Mountain stands a Lady" while one girl skipped. After a while, she would be joined by another. The children also played ball games, hide-and-seek, rounders and tackie (tig). The high jump was known as "High-Low-Leap."

Mr Bews continued as head teacher until the arrival of Mr Harry Smith in 1963. An accomplished violinist, Mr Smith did much to encourage his pupils to appreciate and enjoy music. During his time, the girls won the Scullion Cup for dancing and the boys did very well in the primary schools' football league. The school also reached the finals of the Scots Quiz organised by Ellon Junior Chamber of Commerce.

Mr Smith retired in 1986 and was succeeded by Miss Christine Gilmour in 1987. There were 80 pupils, four full-time teachers and three part-time specialist teachers. Along with other schools in Scotland, a School Board was established in 1988.

Overcrowding was a major problem and in 1996 the whole school

Retirement presentation in 2004 for Mrs Hazel Stuart after 30 years at Cultercullen School. Ellon Times.

2004 Cultercullen School showing the new extension.

relocated to Meiklemill in Ellon to allow the much needed and long-awaited extension to be built. Three new classrooms and a workroom/staff room meant that there was space in the old part of the school for a library and activities such as drama.

Particular thanks to Violet Garrick, Moira Massie, Jeanette Meecham and Hazel Stuart for their help with this section.

On the 23rd of June 1875, the "Aberdeen Daily Free Press" reported how the children of Cultercullen celebrated Queen Victoria's Jubilee.

"The Queen's Jubilee was most successfully celebrated on the Beauty Hill, Foveran, on Tuesday afternoon, when Colonel Hunter of Tillery treated the children attending Culter-Cullen Public School to a picnic and games. The greater number of the children, who numbered not less than 300, started

Cultercullen Football Team 1981.
Photo Cultercullen School.

Beauty Hill.

from school at 1p.m., and marching in procession (except the smaller ones who were conveyed by carts under the able superintendence of Mr. Marr, Ground Officer, Tillery), in charge of Mr. Rose, schoolmaster, arrived on the hill about 2 o'clock.

Immediately on arrival, the children, at the request of Mr. Rose, gave three cheers for Colonel and Mrs Hunter, who were in attendance, and who were on all sides much adored for their personal attention to the little ones.

After the Jubilee hymn had been sung, the children, their parents, and friends, who in all numbered about 450, partook of an excellent tea, purveyed by Mrs Marr. Each one present was, from the hands of Colonel and Mrs Hunter, presented with a Jubilee medal.

The usual games were engaged in, and were ably conducted by Mr. Marr

and Mr. Rose. The weather, which had been warm, with a refreshing northerly wind all afternoon, turned chilly towards eight o'clock, when the children mostly all dispersed, the younger ones being driven home again. This did not, however, by any means finish the games and sport, for the number was well kept up by crowds coming to witness the fire later on.

Music was discoursed under the able leadership of Mr. Mair, Culter-Cullen, and dancing was kept up till within a short time of setting the fire ablaze.

Amongst those present were, Colonel and Mrs Hunter of Tillery, Rev. and Mrs J. S. Loutit, Foveran Parish Church: Mr. Harvey and party from Middlemuir; Mr. and Mrs Marr, Ironrieves; Mr. and Mrs Rose, Schoolhouse, Culter-Cullen; Mr. Fiddes, Auchloon; Mr., Mrs and Miss Merchant, Craibedona; Misses Black, Monkshill; Mr. Burgess, Rennieshill: Mr Gibson, Culter-Cullen; Miss Cooper, Summerhill; Mr. Taylor, baker, Summerhill; Mr. Cooper, Summerhill; Mr. Gray, Culter-Cullen; Mr. and Mrs Dawson, Tillyeve; Misses Reid, Schoolhouse, Craigie.

At 10:30 p.m. a rocket was fired, and in a few seconds Mrs Hunter applied the match to the fire which burned briskly for more than half an hour. Simultaneously with the ignition of this fire were to be seen fires on the top of almost every hill that the eye could scan. From the position of the Beauty Hill there was a most commanding view, and on every side were to be seen demonstrations of loyalty of every description.

The fire which presented the most glaring appearance was that on Brimmond Hill. From there about 30 fires could be numbered and in every quarter were to be seen rockets soaring high into the air. Fireworks of a very beautiful and varied character were displayed on the Beauty Hill."

Until the mid 1990s, Kenny Innes had a business at the west end of Cultercullen making horse boxes then parts for the oil industry.

The Dominie's House.

Duguid's yard on the site of the old smiddy.

The Joiner's House. Photographs courtesy of Cultercullen School.

Prisoners of War from Pitmedden. Alfred Biermann is in the centre in the back row.

Photograph courtesy of Mrs Esson.

During the Second World War there was a large Prisoner of War Camp near Pitmedden. Many of the prisoners worked on local farms. They were taken to their places of work in the morning and picked up again in the evening.

One such prisoner was Alfred Biermann from Bielefeld in Germany who worked at Cultercullen Farm. Alfred was well treated by farmer Alfred Marr and his family and in 1946 sent them a Christmas card containing four watercolours.

He was clearly a skilled artist and the paintings are all the more impressive considering how difficult it must have been for Alfred to find paper and paints just after the war. He finally returned to Germany in March 1948 having been held captive in Britain until then.

Photograph courtesy of Mrs Esson.

164

Monkshill early 20th century.   Photograph courtesy of Charles Esson.

Harry Murray. Hairst at
Cultercullen.
Photograph Charles Esson.

Hairst at Cultercullen 1938.
Photograph Charles Esson.

Photograph courtesy of Bill Johnston.

Hairst at Cultercullen 1938.
Photograph Charles Esson.

UDNY STATION

Udny Station circa 1900.　　　Photograph courtesy of Bill Johnston & Keith Fenwick.

The railway, in the shape of the Formartine and Buchan Railway Company, reached the Parish of Foveran on the 18th of July 1861, when the line from Dyce to Peterhead was opened as far as Mintlaw. The remaining sections from Mintlaw to Peterhead and Maud Junction to Fraserburgh followed on the 3rd of July 1862 and the 24th of April 1865 respectively.

The Formartine and Buchan merged with the Great North of Scotland Railway on the 1st of August 1866, and the Great North itself was absorbed in the London and North East Railway in 1923 which in turn was nationalised as part of British Railways in 1948.

The new railway touched the western edge of Foveran parish on its boundary with the parish of Udny and the station was, a little inaccurately, named Udny. Clearly the promoters of the line saw the new station drawing the bulk of its business from the Udny side of the tracks and identified it accordingly. They would have recognised also that Foveran was already well served by the port of Newburgh and that the greater part of the parish was within easy reach of Aberdeen by the horse drawn vehicles of the day. Even so, the farmers of Foveran shared in the great agricultural boom of the second half of the nineteenth century made possible by the coming of the railways and the new markets which they opened up in the densely populated industrial areas of both Scotland and England.

The present village of Udny Station grew up around the new railway station and became a centre of some local commercial importance, probably reaching its peak in the first half of the twentieth century when, in addition to the station itself, it boasted an hotel, a large general merchant's business, a branch of the North of Scotland Bank, later the Clydesdale, a telephone exchange and Post Office, a garage and, not least, a resident doctor.

As if that list were not impressive enough, some residents of the time might well have pointed also to the service offered by the local grocer just down the road on the Udny side of the railway where a discreet dram might be procured by those in need when the bar of the Station Hotel was closed under the restrictive licensing laws of the day.

The Great North was never what might be described as a flashy railway, unlike some of its neighbours. It did not go in for high speeds, colourful paint jobs or fancy engines but provided an all round, respectable service for the equally respectable inhabitants of the North East.

In the very early days, so far as the Buchan line and Udny were concerned, this meant slow and tedious journeys with most trains being

Showing the branch line. Both trains are heading towards Aberdeen and have come from the Ellon direction. The gentleman is Lewie Gray, the station porter. He has a shunting pole (an implement with a hook at the end for coupling and uncoupling goods wagons) tucked under his arm ready to do the shunting once the loco is detached from the train and moves forward and then reverses back into the goods yard.

Photo G.H. Robin.

"Mixed", that is, conveying goods wagons in addition to passenger coaches with consequent delays at stations while wagons were shunted on and off the trains. The timetable for 1863 shows trains taking anything up to an hour to cover the 14 or so miles from Aberdeen to Udny.

As freight traffic developed, and with greater expertise in operating the railway, it became possible to run separate trains for passenger and goods trains and also for the rapidly expanding fish business from Peterhead and Fraserburgh. Over the years, it became possible to speed up the passenger trains but it should be remembered that "speed" was always a relative term on the Buchan line.

At the height of the railway age, in the years prior to the First World War, Udny enjoyed its best ever passenger service with about six trains a day in each direction and a journey time to and from Aberdeen of about 30 minutes. During the same period, the Great North pioneered a number of bus services in the North East including one to and from Methlick to connect with the trains at Udny.

The bus service was no doubt a much more sensible idea than that of the seventh Earl and first Marquis of Aberdeen who had plans prepared for a branch line from Udny to Methlick via Tarves. The whole line, be it noted, over his own land of which he had some 60,000 acres.

The key figure at the station was, of course, the Agent as the Great North designated its stationmasters. There was William McConnachie from the turn of the century until the late thirties, followed by Alex R. Milne, John Donald, John Flett from 1944-54, and lastly John Munro from 1954-1960.

The stationmasters at Udny were also responsible for the stations at Newmachar and Logierieve but they actually lived in Newmachar from the late thirties onwards although their base was at Udny. Johnnie Flett, at least, got round his extensive area by means of a railway motor cycle. Amazing though it may seem now, he obtained a driving license simply by submitting an application as an "Essential User", there being no driving tests during the Second World War. After a number of misadventures, his wife simply gave thanks that there was little motor traffic in that petrol-rationed era.

After the Second World War, the station staff included John Barrie and Geordie Paterson, the two signalmen who between them operated the signal box from about 4am to 8pm daily. They were both veterans of the First World War and excellent all round railwaymen.

Photograph courtesy of Bill Johnston.

The GNSR bus at Udny Station. The man on the left with the heavy jacket and bonnet (his only protection against the elements) was the driver with the conductor on his left. The two men at the back of the bus are station staff, probably the porter and the clerk.

The GNSR bus service between Udny Station and Methlick ran from 15th November 1904 until 1st January 1907.

The registration number of the bus was SA76 (the 76th vehicle to be registered in Aberdeenshire). It was a Miles-Daimler 16/18 HP chassis no. 1291, and the body was also Miles-Daimler and permanently fixed to the chassis with 18 seats and a rear entrance. It was not unusual in those days for the bodies to be demountable and interchanged between chassis.

The footbridge across the railway in the background was removed sometime between the Wars and passengers had to cross the tracks by a level crossing at the Ellon end of the platforms. Engine drivers were given the following orders: "DOWN PASSENGER TRAINS. The Drivers of all Down Passenger Trains stopping at Udny Station must bring their trains to a stand at the north end of the platform." This was so that the crossing was kept clear for passengers to cross the line in front of the engine. Those of a more nervous disposition waited until the train had left. This was an unusual arrangement and there were very few stations without a footbridge.

Geordie lived in a bungalow he had built himself adjacent to the station and could frequently be seen taking the air with Mrs Paterson in their pony and trap.

John Barrie was a strong minded character sometimes at odds with his opposite number at Ellon, the equally strong minded James R. Davidson, signalman at, and provost of Ellon.

The exchanges between these two men on the signalling telephone system, on which their colleagues could eavesdrop, were sometimes memorable. One long and fruitless debate was alleged to have ended "Aye Aye Barrie, eere aye richt, of coorse". To which the response was "Weel", pause for effect, "Gey often, ye ken."

Porter and general factotum was Lewie Gray. His domain extended to everything outside the office and signal box, particularly the goods shed, Bibby's store, goods yard and platforms. Lewie, a solid citizen, could often be found in off duty hours dispensing beer and wisdom behind the bar of the Station Hotel.

In those pre-computer days of complex double entry book keeping and form filling, the clerks played a considerable part in the smooth running of the station. They were mainly young men learning the railway business and a spell at a station such as Udny could teach them much.

There was also a squad of "Navvies" who maintained the track - Sandy Melvin, the ganger or foreman, who lived at Newmachar, Willie Elrick whose wife kept the level crossing gates at Tillyeve, Andy Greig from Pitmedden and Geordie Smith from Udny Station who was a dab hand at cutting hair when not looking after the rails.

The train passing Tillycorthie is the daily fish train from the Broch.

Udny Station from the south about 1954.   Photograph Douglas Flett.

On the passenger side business could hardly be described as brisk. There was little commuting as is now known with most people living near their place of work. Journeys tended to be "one-offs" for specific purposes. The only regulars were some half dozen school children going to Ellon and perhaps the most interesting were occasional wandering minstrels from the far south destined for the famous Haddo House concerts.

Other customers for the passenger trains were the local poultry dealers, Bobby Smith and Peter Isaac, who loaded their crates of dead birds into the London and Manchester bound guards' vans. They would be joined in season by the tweeded gamie from Haddo despatching consignments of game to the south.

Inwards parcels arrived in large quantities including day-old chicks, homing pigeons for release, calves in sacks, pigs in crates, spares for ploughs and binders and more digestible items such as large cartons of Lyons cakes. There was also what appeared to be a never ending torrent of mail order packages to every cottar house in the surrounding parishes reflecting the popularity of "Clubbie" shopping at the time.

In the days before Tesco, Asda and their rivals, much of the stock in trade of the local shops arrived by rail: flour for the bakers, tea, sugar, jam, sheep dip, netting wire, binder twine and just about everything sold by the country general merchants to say nothing of beer and whisky for the pub.

By the wagon load came draff (the residue from distilling) from Speyside for feeding the dairy kye and a grand whisky smell it made on a frosty morning when shovelled from railway wagon to horse or tractor drawn carts by the fairm billies of whom there might be a dozen loudly

The "Shop" in the 1950s. Next to the shop is what was the Public Hall. Next is the gable of the stationmaster's house, then the block of houses for railway staff.   Photo P&J.

The Station building. Photo Norris Forrest 1960. Courtesy of the Great North of Scotland Railway Association.

exchanging the gossip of the day as they worked. Animal feed for the Bibby's store came from Liverpool and lime and slag for spreading on the parks came from the north of England.

The great bulk of the outwards traffic consisted of seed potatoes, for which the Udny district was famed, to East Anglia and other places in England. In good seasons, surpluses of potatoes would be bought up by the Ministry of Food (as today, no lack of official interference) for pig food. To prevent illicit resale for human consumption, they had to be sprayed with a bright blue dye. Now, for some reason known only to the Ministry, this job - and a messy job it was too - had to be performed by railway staff. The lot usually fell to Lewie Gray who would emerge looking like an ancient Pict painted up in blue war paint and ready to tackle the invading Roman army.

The station staff were very much part of the local community, particularly the village of Udny Station. In charge of the Post Office and also the manual telephone exchange were Barbara and Jimmy Urquhart. Jimmy Moir, his father also a railwaymen, ran the "Shop", known officially as Fraser's Stores, which sold everything conceivable - and what was not conceivable could generally be obtained to order.

Next door was the "Garage" presided over by the genial Bert Lamb who, with Mrs Lamb, played a prominent part in the social life of the village. Doctor Thomson, located in Woodside Terrace, could pull a tooth as readily as write a prescription and had the "Daily Mirror" sent specially from the station bookstall at Aberdeen every day by the 8.20am train. It was rumoured locally that the Doctor took the "Mirror" for the racing tips rather than for the adventures of Jane.

Society had begun to change rapidly in the 1950s and the process was to destroy both the railway and the rural way of life it served. The railway itself, of course, had acted as a violent agent of change only a hundred years before and was now to fall victim in turn. The Beeching axe fell on Udny and the rest of the Buchan line on the 4th of October 1965 when the passenger trains were withdrawn. The goods service followed suit at Udny on the 28th of March 1966, although a goods service of a sort continued to Fraserburgh until 1979. A way of life ended with it.

Douglas Flett.

Douglas Flett was born in Buckie and attended Kennethmont and Newmachar Public Schools and at Robert Gordon's College where he did not distinguish himself. Like his father, he spent his working life as a railwayman. He worked in Aberdeen, York, Glasgow, Newmachar and Udny and retired from the British Railways Board HQ in London, one step ahead of privatisation. He now lives in Nairn and is an enthusiastic member of the G.N.S.R. Association.

Geordie Paterson's bungalow can be seen through the trees. The train is the 'Formartine and Buchan Excursion' operated by the Great North of Scotland Railway Association on 24-05-69 from Aberdeen to Peterhead & Fraserburgh some four years after the last passenger train.

Photograph courtesy of Hazel Stuart.

The south end of the Station in 1969.   Photo courtesy of Keith Fenwick.

George Moir.   Photograph P&J.

The Garage run by Albert Lamb.

When George Moir started work in Fraser's Store in 1928 there were only 47 people living in Udny Station. The shop served not just the village itself but the surrounding countryside as well and sold everything from clothes to furniture to fencing wire.

George took over the shop from his boss Alexander Fraser in 1950 and established the post office in the store four years later. He also had a grocery van which went round the farms in the area. George retired in 1979 after serving the community for fifty one years.

Sadly, the shop closed in 1989 and for two years became a bistro.

The Clydesdale Bank van outside the Bank. The Bank closed in 1985. The van continued for four years after that until it was taken off the road altogether.

James Rollo Duncan, a poor stonemason from New Leeds, went to Bolvia in 1882 where he made his fortune in the tin and silver mines. With his vast wealth, he built not only Tillycorthie House but also many of the substantial granite houses in Udny Station as well.

The Hall, now a grain store, dates from 1915 and was given to the village by Duncan. For many years, dances, whist drives and film shows were held there.

Woodside Terrace and Duncan Terrace were built for the workers in his service on Tillycorthie Estate, the granite brought by rail from the Stirlinghill quarries near Boddam - probably mined by convicts from Peterhead Prison. Duncan was an enlightened and generous benefactor.

Udny Station was the first village in the North East to be lit by electricity thanks to the Duncan Electricity Company.

Tillycorthie House built by Duncan in 1911. This neo-Georgian building was the first in Britain to be built of reinforced concrete.

Duncan built the hall and gave it to the people of Udny Station.

Woodside Terrace built by Duncan for the workers on the estate.

The Ythan Estuary, Aberdeenshire; Kenneth Walton.

The Ythan: a river of history: Dave Raffaelli.

Newburgh-on-Ythan Yesterday and Today. Jessie McPherson.

A Brief History of Foveran Parish Church: Rev. John A. Cook.

Scottish Maritime Records.

The Aberdeen Colliers: Peter Myers. 1987.

Newburgh's Sea-Faring Days: Peter Myers. Leopard June 1977.

The Eastern Counties Aberdeenshire, Angus and Kincardineshire: Nigel Tranter (1972).

The Fortified House in Scotland: Nigel Tranter.

The Statistical Account for Scotland 1791-1799:
Ed. Sir John Sinclair 1982.

The New Statistical Account for Scotland. 1845.

The Third Statistical Account. Chapter 13 vol. 1960.

Fast Sailing and Copper Bottomed: Lucille H. Campey 2002.

Aberdeen Journal Notes and Queries Vol 1 1905.

Constitution and Laws of the Newburgh Shipmasters' Friendly Society 1834.

A Short History of the Shipmaster Society: Alexander Smith. 1911.

For You I Remember: Edith Bishop 1980.

The Early Life of James McBey. An Autobiography.

The Clyack Sheaf: David Toulmin 1986.

View of the Diocese of Aberdeen. Reverend Alexander Keith.

Spalding Club M DCCC XL111.

The Auxiliary Patrol: E. Keble Chatterton. 1923.

The Book of Buchan: Tocher 1910.

The Village When I went to School: Helen Murray.

Shipwrecks of North East Scotland 1444-1990:
David M. Ferguson A.U.P. 1991.

A New History of Aberdeenshire. Ed. Alexander Smith. 1875.

"Fascists in the North East" W. Milne. Leopard Magazine Dec. 1993.

Proceedings of the Society of Antiquaries of Scotland 1908-09.

The Incised Effigial Stone at Foveran, Aberdeenshire:
Neil H. T. Melville.

Aberdeenshire Epitaphs and Inscriptions. Vol 1 John A. Henderson 1907.

The Thanage of Fermartyn: Rev. William Temple. 1894.

Cultercullen School Log Book.

Newburgh Mathers School Log Book.

Foveran School Log Book.

Newburgh Youth Club's Project: Caroline Smith.

Notes on Foveran House. Private papers of Johnston Sangster.

Scottish Development Department. List of Buildings of Architectural or Historical Interest. Area Aberdeen. Sept. 1969.

Newburgh Station 1877-1965: William Guild.

Links with the Past. No 12.

Newburgh Football Club Souvenir Programme 1951.

The Auxiliary Patrol: E. Keble Chatterton 1923.

Aberdeen Notes and Queries. Vol. 1 1908.

Notes on Forvie supplied by Bob Davis.

The Press and Journal Weekend Review Dec.1 1961, Nov. 12 1966, Mar. 3 1973,

The Press & Journal: Dec 18 1967, Mar. 3 1971, Sept 2 1979.

The Ellon Times: Nov. 7 1991.

The People's Journal: Dec. 1945, Nov. 17 1979.

The Aberdeen Journal: Dec. 17 1792, Mar 26 1806, Jul. 18 1877, Dec. 15 1858, Mar. 2 1900, Jan 19 1900, Jul. 6 1908

The Aberdeen Daily Journal : Mar. 13 1900, Jul 6 1908,

The Evening Express Mar. 10 1980, Dec. 16 1988, Apr. 21 1976.

The Banffshire Journal Dec. 8 1964.

Aberdeen Daily Free Press: Jun. 23 1887,

Buchan Observer: Dec. 31 1895.

Peterhead Sentinel & Buchan Journal: Jul. 29 1892, Dec 27 1895.

Perthshire Advertiser Jun. 15 1993.